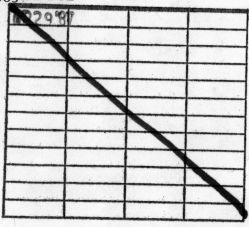

MY
OLYMPIC
YEARS

By the same author

Four Days
Sir Godfrey Kneller and His Times
The Shell Guide to Ireland (with M. V. Duignan)
The Olympic Games: 80 Years of People, Events and Records (with John Rodda)
The Olympic Games: Moscow and Lake Placid (with John Rodda)
The Olympic Games: Moscow and Lake Placid Results

MY
OLYMPIC
YEARS

by
Lord Killanin

William Morrow and Company, Inc.
New York 1983

Library of Congress Catalog Number: 83-61562

ISBN: 0-688-02209-X

Printed in the United States of America

First U.S. Edition

1 2 3 4 5 6 7 8 9 10

BOOK DESIGN BY ALLAN MOGEL

Preface

This is not the definitive story of the Olympic Movement during my connection with it since 1950. That story awaits the historical researcher.

My story is personal. It is, at times, critical of the International Olympic Committee, some of its members, and other groups and individuals that are part of the Olympic Movement, including the international federations, the national Olympic committees, and the organising committees. Where it is critical I accept my own share of culpability, but hope that we can learn from the past and that any criticism will be accepted in the positive manner in which it is intended.

After my election as president of the Olympic Council of Ireland in 1950, little did I think I would be elected president of the International Olympic Committee in 1972. During my eight years in office I travelled nearly one million miles, had contact with about 150 different countries and territories, and visited nearly 100. As a result I have friends, acquaintances, and enemies on all the five continents. It is my hope that the publication of this book will not increase the number of my enemies.

This volume was made possible by my former colleagues on the IOC and the international federations, national Olympic committees, and organising committees. Special thanks go to: Monique Berlioux, the director of the IOC, and the staff of the IOC headquarters in Lausanne for their assistance in checking facts for me; Norma MacManaway, who ran my IOC Dublin office from 1972 to 1980 and assisted me not only in the early stages of writing this volume but throughout my trying eight years of office; Bridget Foley, my secretary from my film-producing days, who helped when necessary during my Olympic presidency as well as on all the drafts of this book; the

5

late David Farrer, who originally suggested the volume, Rivers Scott, and Bill Neill-Hall of Martin Secker and Warburg; Elizabeth Frost Knappman of William Morrow and Company; John Rodda of *The Guardian*, who has acted as a catalyst in reminding me of events that he witnessed as a regular reporter at the Olympic Games and at all meetings of the IOC; and finally my wife, who assisted me in preparing the manuscript, and during my years in office accompanied me to the Games and IOC sessions, making the many problems easier to face.

KILLANIN

Dublin, 1983

Contents

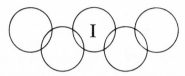

The Flame Goes Out in Moscow

In Moscow on August 3, 1980, I brought to a close my last Olympic Games. One hundred thousand people were crowded into the huge Central Lenin Stadium. The evening was clear and fine, but daylight had gone and the long rigid arms of brilliance from the spotlights had held me since I stepped down from my box, walked across the running track, and mounted the steps of the rostrum, from which I would speak. Athletes and officials were crowded into the arena. Flags of the participating countries and the Olympic Movement were to be everywhere. Yet amid this vast company, I could not but feel lonely. For after eight tough years as president of the International Olympic Committee (IOC), I was saying good-bye.

When I finished my speech the Olympic flame was extinguished to the strains of the Olympic anthem. The Olympic flag was lowered from the main flagpole and carried horizontally across the arena by eight men in uniform. A five-gun salute reverberated through the stadium. Then the choir began to sing.

I returned to the presidential box, where Premier Aleksei Kosygin was sitting. Fatally ill, he was appearing in public for the last time. Together we watched the flag bearers and competitors march out.

Then the flash cards, which had been used with the accuracy common in Eastern European countries throughout the Games, produced a picture of Misha the bear, the mascot of the Moscow celebration, who had succeeded his counterparts Waldi the dachshund of Munich and Anik the beaver of Mon-

9

treal. The flash cards depicted Misha waving good-bye with tears falling from his left eye.

He was symbolising the sadness of the closing of the Games and I too felt close to tears. For politicians had tried to make use of sport and sportsmen for ends they were unable to achieve by political, diplomatic, or economic means. I reflected bitterly on President Jimmy Carter's decision to prevent the United States Olympic team from competing, on then Prime Minister Malcolm Fraser's attempt to force the Australian Olympic Committee to boycott the Games, and on Margaret Thatcher's bid to keep the British team home. The British and Australians had eventually come to Moscow, but the Games had been damaged.

Ninety-five percent of my problems as president of the IOC involved national and international politics. During my eight years in the presidency, I had more crises than my predecessor, Avery Brundage, had in his twenty. In 1972, at the time of the massacre of the Israeli athletes at the Munich Games, I was president-elect, due to assume office as soon as the Games ended. In the two years before 1976 I was very worried over Montreal. First I doubted that the stadium would be ready in time. Then, at the last moment, Canadian Prime Minister Pierre Trudeau refused to allow Taiwan to compete. Finally, African and other countries boycotted the Games because New Zealand's rugby team had played in South Africa earlier that year. Clearly politics are "in" sport and have always been. Everything in our lives is governed by political decisions. We have varying degrees of freedom, but that freedom is obtained by political decision. Yet what we in sport need is the interest and support of politicians, not their interference.

Moscow, however, was different. The boycott, had it succeeded, would have broken the Olympic Movement. It did not succeed, but at the same time nobody won, and the politicians lost face. Many athletes forfeited their one and only chance of competing in the greatest and most challenging sporting contest in the world. The Games themselves, though brilliantly organised, were fundamentally sad. There were too many faces absent, too many doubts on the part of those who were there.

In the context of sport and of the Olympic Games in particular, the invocation of a country's political misdeeds to justify reprisals is always double-edged. The Soviets claim they were "invited" into Afghanistan; the 1976 Winter Games were allotted to Denver (which, however, later resigned its claim) in 1970, in the middle of America's involvement in the Far East. Who knows what the international situation will be when the time for the next Games to open in Los Angeles arrives in 1984. There are good, sound, practical reasons, as well as moral ones, for dissuading politicians from using sport as a means to an end.

Baron Pierre de Coubertin, founder of the modern Olympic Movement, once wrote: "Athleticism can occasion the most noble passions or the most vile. . . . One can use it to consolidate peace or to prepare for war." The governments backing the boycott were certainly using the Moscow Games—but for what purpose and to what effect? Many of the athletes prevented from taking part still greatly resent the ban. The boycott produced a division within sport between right and left. People were obliged to fly their political colours in circumstances that were alien to them.

The crisis over the Moscow Olympics not only affected the athletes and their national Olympic committees, it also created an unwelcome division among their backers. Unwilling to offend their governments, many large industrial companies chose not to subscribe to their national Olympic funds. Some British trade unions, for opposite reasons, organised special fund-raising efforts. A woeful development in an activity meant for all.

Yet the Games took place, and the day after their closing I handed over a symbolic key to Juan Antonio Samaranch of Spain, who had been elected to succeed me as president. I then flew back to Ireland with feelings of great relief that the strain I had been under since the previous Christmas, when the Afghanistan situation arose, was now at an end.

I also recalled my many satisfactions as president. Foremost among these was getting the People's Republic of China into the Olympic Movement and seeing her athletes compete at Lake Placid, although they were not to compete in my time with the Chinese from Taiwan. Both, unfortunately, did not go to Moscow.

It had been my intention to leave the IOC on a sound financial footing. When I was senior vice-president in the period before Munich, we were living on borrowed money from the television contracts due as a result of the Munich Games. I did accomplish that, for with the sums from Lake Placid and Moscow and the early payments coming through from Los Angeles, before my retirement the IOC was solidly in the black. In December 1972, the IOC had assets of $2,084,290; in December 1980, assets totaled $45,142,752.21, and they have increased under my successor.

I had also promoted the work of the IOC's Medical Commission and lost no chance to warn of the danger to sport and to the athletes themselves of drugs, blood transfusions, and the "artificial man," a concept completely opposed to the Olympic ideal of the complete and true human being.

I thought also of my failures. I would have liked to have seen the Olympic programme restricted, whereas in fact it grew. I would have liked to have seen women elected to the IOC in my time, rather than in my successor's as has happily been the case. Finally, I have to admit complete defeat in my attempts to make the spirit of the Games less nationalistic.

I thought of the good things that had happened to me in those eight years—the friends I had made, the new places I had seen, the firsthand knowledge I had been able to gain in the most agreeable circumstances. Most of all, I thought of the athletes, whom the Olympic Movement exists to serve, and who are the sufferers when politicians manipulate sport.

My predecessor declared that the Olympic Games are "the greatest social force of our time." They are a force indeed—and not one with which to tamper.

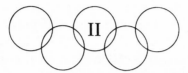

The IOC: Its Growth and Responsibilities

One of the greatest mysteries surrounding the Olympic Games is their operation: how it works, who does what, and why. In the second half of the twentieth century it is difficult to comprehend that the power of such an organisation is retained by a group of people whose existence is "undemocratic." The ultimate power and authority are held by the International Olympic Committee, which Baron Pierre de Coubertin formed when he revived the Games in 1894. The members are the custodians of a trust that he established to ensure that others correctly carried out the work needed to stage the Games and maintained the principles and rules of the Olympic Movement. Trusteeship was at the heart of Coubertin's ideal, though that is not to say that members of the committee have always carried out their trust in the way he would have wished.

The IOC is a self-electing, self-perpetuating body. It is a club in which membership is by invitation, with the unusual exclusivity that there are only one or two people from any one country; in fact, for more than half the world's countries there are no members. Members are not representing their country at the IOC, but the IOC in their country or territory.

What puzzles many people is how liberals like myself and, above all, members of the Communist bloc countries can tolerate such a system. I think we would all answer (perhaps for different reasons) that it would be wrong to shun the responsibility of the power that the Olympic Movement wields.

When Coubertin gathered distinguished sporting people at the Sorbonne in Paris on June 23, 1894, he was thirty-one years old and had for the past ten years been working on the concept of reviving the Olympic Games held in ancient Greece. It had been hoped he would follow the family tradition of a career in the Army, but he had turned from this, and from an early political career, to a more practical way of helping his country. Concerned about the health of the youth of France, he had been comparing the country's attitude toward sport and exercise with that of Britain, Germany, Sweden, and other European countries.

Since the intellectuals of the university had always been opposed to sport on the British model, it is surprising that Coubertin should have selected the Sorbonne as the meeting place for the congress, but the choice of venue proved excellent. Seventy-nine delegates, together with representatives of forty-nine sports associations, came together from twelve countries. To create the right atmosphere, the "Hymn to Apollo," recently discovered in Delphi, was sung at the beginning to music composed for the occasion, for, as always in Coubertin's enterprises, protocol was important and the stage management impeccable.

The international committee then created was entrusted with the control and development of the modern Olympic Games, which were held for the first time in Athens in 1896. Originally the committee was a very informal body. Coubertin took his model from the Henley Royal Regatta in England, which is run by invited officials (stewards) with a management committee. Unlike the Olympic Games, Henley has not changed much since the late nineteenth century and the quality and efficiency of its organisation might have been a continuing lesson for the Olympic Movement. In the early days the IOC had fifteen members, which had increased to forty-eight by the eve of the First World War; today there are over eighty. Until 1915 the headquarters were in Paris, but when Coubertin moved to Lausanne, Switzerland, he took the organisation with him and it has remained there ever since.

The IOC's original, simple framework had many advantages but, as the years passed, it became increasingly inadequate to deal with the many and complex problems that had to be faced—for example, demands from other organisations, from cities wanting to stage the Games, from sports wanting a place on the Olympic programme, and from those already on the programme demanding more events; the needs and competition of television; and the advantages that the world of commerce and business saw in being associated with the movement.

In addition to the IOC, the structure of the Olympic family comprises the national Olympic committees (NOCs), which every country or territory must have to send a team to the Games; the international federations (IFs) for sports on the Olympic programme; and the cities staging the Games. At the moment there are over 150 national Olympic committees, which have recently formed their own world group and have several geographical organisations as well. Twenty-nine sports are on the programme and now, with the time it takes to prepare for the Games, four cities (currently Los Angeles and Sarajevo, Yugoslavia, for 1984 and Seoul, South Korea,* and Calgary, Canada, for 1988) are recognised and in consultation with the IOC. All these groups have grown and developed in procedures and power over the past fifty years, while the IOC has only recently changed. By the very nature of this growth, much responsibility has had to be passed on from the IOC either to groups within the Olympic family or to organisations outside (such as television), and some are not always as keen in their pursuit of upholding the Olympic principles as the IOC would wish them to be. It is like a tug-of-war in which at times the IOC looks like a hopeless loser; but, whatever the changes, however often people and organisations break the rules, the original concept of Coubertin's trusteeship must be maintained. It is the ultimate source of Olympic power.

The IOC's most important administrative responsibilities are choosing the cities for the Games, ensuring they follow Olympic rules, recognising and supporting the NOCs' and IFs' rights, and selecting new IOC members, as well as negotiating television rights.

---

* The Olympic Movement does not officially employ the terminology of "North" and "South" for the Koreas or "East" and "West" for the Germanys; the terms have been used in this book solely for the sake of easy understanding.

Among the principal aims of the IOC are the following:

To encourage the organisation and development of sport and sports competitions.

To inspire sports within the Olympic ideal, thereby promoting the strengthening of friendship between sportsmen of all countries.

To ensure the regular celebration of the Olympic Games.

To make the Olympic Games even more worthy of their glorious history and the high ideals which inspired their revival.

Rule 3 of the IOC charter now reads:

The Olympic Games take place every four years. They unite Olympic competitors of all the countries in fair and equal competition.

The International Olympic Committee (IOC) shall secure the widest audience for the Games.

No discrimination in them is allowed against any country or person on grounds of race, religion or politics.

The position of the IOC president is powerful. With the members meeting only once a year, or twice during the year of the Games, much of the day-to-day implementation of policy is in his hands, with the director of the IOC carrying it out from the headquarters in Lausanne at the Château de Vidy. The Executive Board is the policy-making body, and that now meets two or three times a year. Ultimately jurisdiction rests with the IOC members, who can overrule decisions made by the president or the board except when, as the IOC has often been asked to do, it undertakes a special task.

The selection of new IOC members essentially rests with the president and Executive Board, and rarely is there open opposition to a nomination; in turn, the IOC elects the president and board. While IOC members remain such until they resign, retire, or die, the president is elected for a period of eight years. He may subsequently be reelected for periods of four years. It is under this reelection system that Brundage was president for twenty years. I had always stated that it was my intention to take office for one term, i.e., eight years. The period of two Olympiads seems to me sufficient for a president to see the problems in his first Olympiad and remedy many of them in the second. After that he can be *in situ* too long.

The Executive Board members are proposed and seconded and subject to an election whenever vacancies occur. The statutory term for a member of the board is four years. However, should he die or be promoted (to president or vice-president, for instance) in the first year of office, another member can be elected to fill the vacancy for the balance of the term and is eligible to be a candidate for reelection. It is therefore possible for a member of the Executive Board, under these circumstances, to be in office for seven years.

Unfortunately, the rules have not always been closely followed. The requirement that all members should speak either French or English was ignored in 1951, a year before my own election, by the election and admission of the first Soviet member, Constantin Andrianov, who spoke only Russian and had to have an interpreter. Andrianov has been a very loyal member of the IOC, but his linguistic limitations were an undoubted drawback and the introduction of his private interpreter represented a crucial change.

In my early days as a member, the headquarters staff consisted only of a part-time chancellor, Otto Mayer, who owned an exclusive jewellery shop in Lausanne and ran the IOC's business, with the aid of a part-time secretary, from the back room of his premises and the bar of the next-door hotel. Now, with the many and complex tasks that confront them, the multinational staff numbers more than thirty, and while French and English (with French taking precedence) are still the only official languages, Spanish, Russian, German, and the language of the country hosting the proceedings are used at full sessions of the IOC with all the apparatus of simultaneous translation. This multiplication of languages, inevitable though it may be, has in subtle ways altered the character of the meetings. French- and English-speakers can, by nuance and tone, convey through diplomatic phrasing much more than often is done by translators. The latter, despite their best efforts in a demanding role, have brought a brittleness to the IOC debates, which were never of a very high standard anyway.

In recent years the IOC has become involved in many

technical areas where expert knowledge is required, such as medicine, television, and the press. Setting up commissions involving experts in these fields, together with a few members of the IOC, NOCs, and IFs, has generated more detailed information on various aspects of the Games.

The Olympic rules state that there shall be only one member of the IOC for any one country, but in the case of the largest and most active countries in the Olympic Movement, and those in which the Olympic Games have been held, there can now be a maximum of two. Actually, when I was first elected, many countries had three members; these included Britain, France, the United States, and China. According to the rules, members are not allowed to accept instructions from their government or any organisation or individual that in any way bind them or interfere with the independence of their vote. For this reason the original members were all persons of independent means, though unfortunately independence of means does not always mean independence of thought.

The IOC has been described as the "most exclusive club in the world." At the time of my election in 1952 there was one head of state (the reigning Prince Francis Joseph II of Liechtenstein), three other princes (Axel of Denmark, Jean of Luxembourg, now the grand duke, and Pierre of Monaco), and one archduke (Mecklenburg of Germany). There were three counts, five peers (which my election raised to six), three knights or ritters, a pasha, a rajah, and a host of people who had held high positions and were entitled to the prefix of "His Excellency" or "the Honourable." Members were expected to pay their own expenses, as well as a subscription to the IOC, as is the custom in any club.

There is no longer a subscription, and that is something I regret. The IOC now pays the members' basic travelling expenses, and many IFs and NOCs also make contributions. Though this is a step forward, the discipline and commitment of paying a club subscription ought to have been maintained.

The selection for membership of the IOC over the years should not be underestimated. The majority are of the highest integrity and greatly respected in their own countries. Many have been presidents of their national Olympic committees, or

Olympic competitors and medallists. The late marquess of Exeter, who as Lord Burghley won for Britain a gold medal at Amsterdam in 1928 and a silver four years later in Los Angeles; Sir Arthur Porritt (now Lord Porritt) of New Zealand; King Constantine of the Hellenes; Julian Roosevelt of the United states; Masaji Kiyokawa of Japan; Peter Tallberg of Finland; and Pirjo Haggman of Finland, who was among the first women to be elected—all were Olympic competitors of distinction.

Originally the members nominated their successors and these nominations were usually accepted. This led to "family seats" in the IOC, and in the years following my election sons, sons-in-law, and nephews of former members contributed greatly to the movement, but this has its obvious dangers.

I do not believe the IOC should be criticised for what might appear to be an hereditary system, *if* the candidates are suitable. It is a system common to all walks of life and society—to democracies as well as totalitarian states of both the left and the right. It is safer to select someone who is known than someone who is unknown.

There have been problems with members of royal families who suddenly become *persona non grata* in their own countries because of a change in regime. King Constantine left Greece and resigned his IOC membership in exile but, as befitted an Olympic gold medallist, was made an honorary member. He still maintains a close interest in IOC affairs. Prince Gholam Reza Pahlavi of Iran, the brother of the late shah, was a member and fled the country when the regime was overthrown. For a long time we did not know the whereabouts of the prince, but I eventually made contact and he, too, resigned.

The IOC members attempt to conduct their business on a democratic basis and a decision once made is binding on all. It is impossible to do business without collective responsibility and if a member cannot stomach a policy it is open to him to resign.

A member may resign for whatever reasons at any time, but since 1965 there has been a rule that anyone elected after that year must resign at the end of the calendar year in which he attains the age of seventy-two. This will eventually reduce the average age, although some of the best members are active in their seventies and even beyond. We lost General Sven Tho-

felt of Sweden, president of the modern pentathlon association, under this rule. On the other hand, one of my most valuable members, Herman van Karnebeek of Holland, resigned voluntarily on exceeding seventy-two to make room for a younger man. The rule was introduced with the best intentions and no exceptions have been made, though a member can continue as president or vice-president, or on the Executive Board, until the end of his term. An attempt to extend the age to seventy-six was made at the session in Rome in 1982, but failed. Further attempts may be made, especially when the majority of members come under the rule, but it would of course exacerbate the geriatric image of the IOC.

A member may be expelled: my predecessor as president, Avery Brundage, had to ask one member to resign on the grounds of his unsuitability. Brundage himself was elected to the IOC in place of Ernest Lee Jahncke, member for the United States, who was removed when he opposed the participation of the American team in the Berlin Games in 1936.

One aspect of the rules that has been misunderstood concerns gifts. Token gifts of friendship are one thing. Bribes, or attempts to curry favour, are quite another. But the line between them can be thin, and, moreover, affected by the customs of the countries concerned.

Once, before I became president, Key Young Chang, a South Korean member, sent a representative to see me in my hotel room in Lausanne. This emissary announced that he knew I had a problem paying my expenses (which was not the case, I assured him) and that Chang wished to give me a present. He held out an envelope. I refused to accept it. "Oh," he said casually, "it's only a thousand dollars." I was much disturbed and told Brundage of the occurrence. He, too, was deeply shocked. Surprising as it may seem, I am convinced that no favour was being sought, but it did put me in a difficult position.

After I became president the presents became an added problem. To most sessions I would travel with nine or ten suitcases and return with thirteen, my wife having hastily gone on an extra shopping expedition for the additional bags to ensure that the many gifts I had received were all safely packed and brought back either to Dublin or Lausanne.

On the eve of my election to the presidency, the members of the IOC were spread more widely geographically than before, although Europe still predominated with thirty-seven members. The next largest representation belonged to North and South America with eighteen members, while the continents of Africa and Asia remained comparatively underrepresented.

During my term of office as president I felt that there should be broader representation on the IOC, especially among the developing countries, and that the NOCs should be consulted to make certain that, like all ambassadors, the members selected were *persona grata* in their respective countries. This did, of course, present the danger that NOCs might eventually gain the power to effectively "elect" members, and so I found myself a target for criticism and opposition. Yet this consultation was necessary, particularly with the newer national committees where we still had few contacts. Today things are different. Most members of the IOC have now, like myself, been presidents of NOCs or very closely associated with them or with sports administration generally, or they have been Olympic competitors.

In spite of criticism that the IOC consists of arrogant old aristocrats, I am convinced that Coubertin was far-seeing when he decided that the Olympic Movement should be run by trustees and not by a democratic body, subject to all the problems that nowadays face the United Nations and UNESCO. Communist critics in particular should reflect that if the IOC had been such a body it is highly unlikely that the 1980 Games in Moscow would have taken place.

The IOC has not, in my time, progressed as quickly as it might have done, nor been properly fitted for the changes going on in the world, and not just those of sport. From 1952 to 1972, when Avery Brundage was president, the IOC did little more than mark time and protect itself. These were costly years, and the political problems and traumas that faced me in my presidency took from me much of the time I would have preferred to spend renewing the movement.

The IOC was particularly behind in understanding the potential of television. No one grasped quickly enough the value, or the danger, that this medium held for the Games and their development. The first Games to be televised were those of Berlin in 1936, when events were shown on large screens in a few places. In 1948 only a few sets in Britain were able to receive a transmission, but the limited coverage during the 1950's ought to have alerted the IOC to the potential for growth. The first realistic commercial sales of rights were made for the Winter Games in Squaw Valley, California, in 1960. But even in 1968, when the Mexican organisers had a contract worth $4 million with ABC, the IOC was not a party to it and was given a pittance of $150,000. Even after that, organising committees were left with too much freedom in negotiating television rights, but I am glad to see that my successor is ensuring a full partnership with Seoul and Calgary when they come to consider the television contracts for the Games of 1988, which may generate revenues of over $500 million.

Of course, with vast sums from television going into the Games, some of the federations have made unreasonable technical demands—for example, the late Ingrid Frith, president of the International Archery Federation, wanted "lawns like Wimbledon tennis courts" over which the arrows were to fly in Moscow. Needless to say they were not; perfectly ordinary grass works just as well.

While I was aware of the need to cooperate with the federations and to ensure that technical excellence in the arrangements for their sports was achieved, I knew that television, and the funds it brought in, was a compelling part of their need to stay within the movement. The publicity given to minor sports through the televised Games was enormous; the growth of judo, volleyball, gymnastics, and basketball in such countries as Britain came about in this way, just as did the growth of track and field in Japan, where it had been a relatively minor sport. In this way television has played an extraordinary part in binding the Olympic family together. If there had not been this magnetism, the frustrations some of them suffered in the sixties might well have brought about a splintering of the movement.

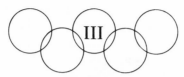

An Olympic Start

My Olympic life began not through any prowess at sport, but by trying to resolve disputes and squabbles. Ireland was not only divided politically, with the Six Counties part of the United Kingdom, but in sport too. Some sports presented a united Irish team, while others were without the North. Within Ireland itself there were divisions, with two organisations in cycling, track and field, and other sports, each claiming to represent the country at an international level. With the resurgence of sport after the war, many Irish sportsmen were concerned about these damaging divisions. Two of the country's leading boxing administrators, Major General W.R.E. Murphy, former president of the International Amateur Boxing Association, and Patrick Carroll, president of the Irish Amateur Boxing Association, were among those who wanted sense and order in the situation.

Murphy was from the North. He had fought in the First World War and been awarded the Distinguished Service Order and Military Cross. He then joined the Irish Free State Army, before transferring to the newly formed Irish Civic Guards. Carroll had been a member of the old Irish Republican Army and subsequently joined the Irish Free State Army. He also transferred to the Irish Civic Guards, working in the Special Branch during and after the war. They came to me asking that I become president of the Olympic Council of Ireland because they believed I would be acceptable to "both sides."

The Olympic Council of Ireland is an all-Ireland body. I

was already known to be sympathetic to the idea of a united Ireland in politics, business, and sport. I had also been involved in a group of people of all political parties and faiths working to obtain the release of IRA prisoners, some of whom had been imprisoned by the British since the incidents in London in 1938 and 1939, when a favourite occupation was the blowing-up of pillar boxes. It was at this time that the future playwright Brendan Behan, later to become a friend of mine, was sent to Borstal, the reformatory prison.

My sympathy with their cause but not all their methods made me acceptable to the nationalist Irish. From the Northern Protestant point of view my soundness was established by the fact that I had said I would volunteer to fight Nazism if war broke out, and had indeed joined the British Territorial Army after the Munich crisis of 1938. All of this made me suspect to extremists on both sides but acceptable to all other shades of opinion.

In sport I had the example of the Irish Amateur Boxing Association, which, thanks to the influence of Murphy, Carroll and others, has long been run successfully on an all-Ireland basis, as are the majority of sports; in fact, one of its vice-presidents, back in the 1950's, was a captain of the Royal Ulster Constabulary. I wished to heal the political split in Irish track and field and in cycling; in that endeavour I failed, although obtaining a compromise in cycling.

My first meeting of the Olympic Council of Ireland was on July 21, 1951, when the invitation to the Games at Helsinki, the following year, was accepted; it is Olympic protocol that the invitation to take part comes from the host city. In October I was nominated as delegate to a meeting of national Olympic committees that was going to be held during the time of the 1952 Winter Games in Oslo. I was able to give my council colleagues some good news: after talks with Irish Prime Minister Eamon De Valera, government financial assistance would be available for competitors going to the Games, so long as we matched it pound for pound.

By that time I had become an IOC member. Such rapid promotion came about in this way. Towards the end of 1951, Lord Burghley wrote to me about a vacancy that had occurred on the IOC. J. J. Keane, the first president of the Olympic Council of Ireland, had been elected to the IOC in 1922, having been active in the administration of sport in Ireland. But he had lost interest and failed to attend IOC meetings; consequently his membership had lapsed.

I had known Burghley before the war when I was on the diplomatic staff of the *Daily Mail* and he was a member of Parliament—from my point of view a most useful one as far as information was concerned. After receiving his letter, I met him at my London club, the Garrick, in the back room, then known as "Seymour Hicks's office"—named after the actor who used it most days for the conduct of his business, strictly against club rules. We sat by the fireplace having a drink and Burghley asked me whether I would be interested in being elected a member of the IOC. I replied that, as president of the Olympic Council of Ireland, I naturally knew there was now a vacancy and would be honoured to accept. He explained to me the details and responsibilities of the post and said that my name would come forward at the IOC session to be held before the Winter Games in Oslo.

The work of that session started after its formal opening by the king of Norway. I was summoned to take my seat among the members, although I could neither speak nor vote at this time. I was invited to take a place at the back of the room, since there was nowhere else to sit. From there I watched the enormous Swede, IOC President Sigfrid Edström, control the meeting. He had his walking stick on the table and when he wanted attention he banged it. He told me later that, as president of the International Amateur Athletic Association (IAAF, which governs track and field), he had disliked Ireland and the troubles it brought him over the various splits in the track and field associations. For example, the Irish National Athletic Association had appeared at one IAAF meeting and, while the official languages were French and English, insisted on speaking Irish to the Swedish president.

After that came the 1952 Winter Games themselves. Because I am Irish and had spent so much time in England, I had never before seen any winter sport. For me sport in winter meant fox hunting, shooting, and the steeplechase, not skiing.

Not for the first time in the history of Olympic events, there was a shortage of snow and the Army had to transport snow up many of the slopes because artificial snow had not yet been developed. The ski jump at Holmenkollen, a winter sport centre long before the Oslo Games, was magnificent, however.

I felt at home in Oslo, Norway being the country of Ibsen, whose plays I had first seen at the Festival Theatre, Cambridge. I still have a nineteenth-century Norwegian pipe that I bought then. It gave me the feeling of being a nineteenth-century litterateur.

After the Games we left for home via Sweden and Denmark. An immigration official at the frontier between Norway and Sweden asked to see our passports and said, *"Sprechen Sie Deutsch?"* to which we replied, "No, we speak English." He then said, "Well, you speak very good English for Irish people."

After Sweden and Denmark we intended to travel through Allied-occupied Germany and on to The Hague. At the frontier station we were told we could not pass through as we had no visas to enter Germany. If we had had British passports, it was explained to us, there would have been no problem. We found this ironic in view of the part that my wife and I had played in the war. My wife, for most of the war years, had worked in England on the "Ultra" project, helping to break the German coding system. It was for this work that she was awarded the Order of the British Empire. So I said to one official, "Last time I came to Germany it was easier because I arrived in a tank and not as a private citizen by train."

As a member of the IOC and as president of the Irish NOC, I went with our Olympic team to Helsinki in July 1952. Travelling by train along the coast of the Gulf of Finland we had to pass through the area occupied by Soviet troops. The Iron Curtain had been lowered. At one stage the train had iron shutters screwed against the windows so that we could not look out.

At the opening ceremony of the Helsinki Summer Games, a lady burst into the arena and ran round it in a flowing Grecian robe. For a moment people thought this was some new sort of ceremony, but it was actually the first "demonstration" that I saw in the Olympic arena. I am sure the lady wished to convey some message of peace, but I don't think anyone discovered what it was.

Then the great Finnish runner of the twenties, Paavo Nurmi, winner of nine Olympic gold medals, carried the flame into the stadium. I was impressed by the sight of this almost legendary sportsman, no longer as lean as in the days when he could run the rest of the world off its feet, yet many other members of the IOC were incensed that the Finns had used him for this focal point to the opening ceremony. They considered Nurmi a professional and thus unfitted to carry the sacred flame on the last stage of its journey. At the prompting of the IOC in 1931 and 1932, the International Amateur Athletic Federation had disqualified him for alleged professionalism. Had he run in the marathon at the 1932 Games in Los Angeles he would almost certainly have won another medal. He was later reinstated in Finland for domestic competition and he remained forever a national sporting figure. A statue of him stands outside the Olympic Stadium in Helsinki.

This was my first encounter with the IOC's being behind the times. Nurmi had made a vast contribution to the Olympic Movement and to athletics through his running, and was an inspiration, properly revered by his countrymen and many others throughout the world. Whether he was guilty of professionalism or not I cannot say. When you are an international sportsman of his standing and popularity, drawing large crowds to watch you, then there are bound to be enormous sums of money generated. The temptation to take more than legitimate expenses has always been great, particularly for young people who have not made much headway in their careers. Those who offer money are not within the jurisdiction of the IOC. Is not some, if not all, of the blame to be put on society and specifically the sports bodies whose rules and regulations are restrictive in this area? The socialist world has something to teach the capitalists in this respect.

Indeed, at my first two IOC meetings the organisation broke its own rules in two respects. At Oslo a second member for the Soviet Union was elected and, like the first, he spoke neither English nor French. But more important, perhaps, was the agreement by the Committee at Helsinki to the request of the Soviet team and other countries from the Eastern bloc, competing for the first time since the war, that they have their own Olympic Village as they did not wish to be "contaminated" by the West. The argument to concede to these conditions was a need for this part of the world to be brought back into the Olympic family. Happily this blunder was not repeated at Melbourne or ever again.

The Soviet member elected in Oslo was Aleksei Romanov, and one of the Nordic papers reported that Romanov had been elected for Ireland and "Kalinin" for the Soviet Union. I presume the reporter thought that no one with a surname as czarist-sounding as Romanov could have been selected for the USSR. My own name has frequently been the subject of jokes: Kalinin Prospekt in Moscow, named after the first president of the Supreme Soviet, was jokingly renamed Killanin Prospekt before the 1980 Games by my friends in the IOC.

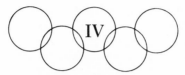

Small Is Beautiful

"Who's won?" I asked, just wanting the reassurance that my eyes had not played tricks. "Your man," replied Prince Philip from the row in front. Here, in 1956, at Melbourne, small was indeed beautiful. These were the last Games before the Olympic Movement appeared worldwide on television, assuming more complexity than ever before. And here was a man from a small country—my country—winning the blue ribbon of the track, the 1,500 metres. As the prince, who had earlier opened the Games on behalf of the queen, and the IOC members around me shared my excitement, Ronnie Delany dropped to his knees, just beyond the finishing line, in prayerful thanksgiving.

Melbourne, on the wrong side of the world as far as the epicentre of the Olympic Movement was concerned, was bound to have a smaller representation for the Games. In Helsinki four years previously, which provides a better example for comparison, there were 7,500 competitors and 1,863 officials, including representatives of the press and other media. At Moscow the organising committee calculated, before the boycott, that there would be 14,000 competitors and 7,300 media personnel alone, an enormous growth in a quarter of a century.

If Melbourne ended an era, there were signs of the coming change and Delany and I represented part of that change. Delany came to the Olympic arena not directly from Ireland but through Villanova University in the United States, to which he had won a scholarship. Many of these scholarships were frowned upon at the time as being awarded purely for athletic ability; some felt that the recipients were if not pseudoprofessionals, then the capitalist equivalent of state-aided athletes.

Yet without Villanova and Jim Elliott, its renowned coach, I doubt whether Delany would have mounted the winner's rostrum in Melbourne. Neither would he, as a result of his education in America, have gone on to his present executive position in the British and Irish Steampacket Company. I would not have been in Melbourne either but for commercial involvement. I could not have afforded to fly to Melbourne and back and I would not have wanted to use any of the Irish Olympic funds. But, as I was an Irish director of Aspro Nicholas, the international pharmaceutical company, at the time, I was able to combine a business trip, visiting plants in Karachi and Bombay on the way. In effect, Delany the competitor and Killanin the administrator were being supported, subsidised, in their Olympic endeavours. So too were many other Olympic competitors, and it worried me that the movement was not, at that time, taking proper account of the situation. Neither did it for many years even after television, increased commercialism, and nationalism took a greater hold.

I was in Melbourne with dual responsibility as president of the Irish NOC and a member of the IOC and, since the Irish team had but twelve members (the equestrian events, in which Ireland is always strong, were held in Stockholm that year), only one official went with it. He was Chris Murphy, who unfortunately fell ill soon after his arrival, leaving the team with no administrator except for the Australian attaché. I found myself commuting between IOC meetings and the Olympic Village before the Games and trying to help out during the events with all kinds of items such as transportation, training, and tickets for the sports. Arthur MacWeeney, the only Irish sportswriter at the Games, also pitched in.

There were high hopes that Delany would get to the finals. In the team quarters before the semifinals, we talked about his chances; his placid attitude and belief that he could win the gold impressed me. He did not want any special treatment, just peace in which to concentrate on the greatest race of his life.

After the excitement of the victory I went down to the

locker room and found the same Delany I had talked to in the Village—quiet, unexcited about it all as though it were not a great achievement. As the evening newspapers were announcing IT'S IRELAND'S GOLD, we celebrated his victory over a beer in my hotel room.

Delany was one of the early four-minute milers. After pursuing his career, he turned to honorary (i.e., unpaid) sports administration in Ireland. So many sportsmen in the Western world, devoting much time to their training and competition, are bound to neglect their working life. They have a lot of catching-up to do once their international sporting days are over, and thus many are lost to the administration of sport.

The thought of those intimate early days still gives me pleasure. In recent years Mexico, Munich, Montreal, and Moscow have all benefited from the Olympic Games by gaining either public housing or transport systems, which might never have been available to their people otherwise. But the Helsinki Games, the first I attended, had to make do with efficiently run existing constructions.

At the previous Games, in London in 1948, immediately after the war, this was even more true. There were building restrictions and only sites that had been cleared after the bombing and buildings, such as Wembley Stadium, that had been constructed many years before the war were available. Time was short and there was no demand by athletes, federations, NOCs, the IOC, or the media for extravagant facilities. At Melbourne, the last of the Games to be intimate and personal, everything except the rowing and yachting took place within easy reach of the city centre. No special stadium was built, but the Melbourne Cricket Club ground was converted temporarily for the occasion, a little more accommodation was constructed, and existing facilities were put to use.

I also recall from those early years how light were the demands that the IOC made on the organising committee for the Games as regarded its own comfort. In 1952 Helsinki was a small city. IOC members had free passes for the buses and all of us, except the president, travelled in this manner to sporting events. Today all IOC members insist on having their own individual car during the Games. For some eighty members to each have a car places an added burden on the resources of the hosts, who also have to provide transport for the numerous teams, competitors, and officials. More recently international federation heads and NOC heads have also had cars. All these are provided by a national car manufacturer, or agent, which means that the officials of the Olympic Movement are subsidised by commercial advertising.

At Helsinki, an extreme formality still reigned. At the innumerable receptions white ties, orders, and decorations were worn, though at least top hats and tails, which had been *de rigueur* before the war, were abandoned for the opening ceremony. Instead, we were issued little badges to put on our jackets or blazers in order to achieve some semblance of uniformity. In those days the members of the IOC left their stand and formed a circle before the presidential or royal box and must have looked ridiculous—a motley crew of varying ages. I was the youngest at thirty-seven except for Prince Jean of Luxembourg. Now the IOC members do not leave the stand.

It would be twenty more years before I was elected president. But long before that I was to become acquainted with two of the forces that have come more and more to darken the idealism inspired by Coubertin and put the whole Olympic Movement at risk: politics and violence.

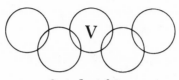

South Africa

Most of the world holds strong objections to South Africa's apartheid laws, but few understand how they have bedevilled the Olympic Movement and the wider sporting world. In South Africa the white minority has imposed its will upon nonwhites to determine that each group will develop separately, ensuring that the laws of the country are finely structured to that end.

The situation is complex. First, a large number of whites are unaware of the standard of living of the nonwhite population, which varies enormously. This is because the black and coloured areas are barred to whites unless they have a permit. Nonwhites can go into white areas to work but not to live, because they are controlled by a pass system. White people living in comfortable, if not luxurious, surroundings find it convenient not to look too closely at how the vast majority of the country survives.

It is an obnoxious system more and more brought to the attention of the world through sport, because the white South Africans, in a country with an ideal climate, are sports mad. The isolation brought about by the IOC in 1970 has brought change but not total respect for human dignity.

For those who wish to see the system changed, the sporting lever has been a convenient tool. The South African question, beginning with my visit there as chairman of an IOC commission in 1967, has been a burden for me and the Olympic Movement. Yet I often wonder whether without sport and specifically the Olympic Games, on which politicians and governments can so easily ride, the bloodshed that many forecast as the only solution might not have come about already.

In principle, the International Olympic Committee really did not need a rule banning discrimination on grounds of race, colour, or religion. Many sportsmen and -women already did not wish to compete against members of a South African team, which came from a country where there were not equal opportunities for all to win a place on that team. In the middle and late fifties there was disquiet about the situation as it related to sport in South Africa and, after long, agonising, and repetitive debate, the IOC closed the door on the country at a meeting in May of 1970 in Amsterdam. South Africa's recognition was withdrawn and it has been outside the movement ever since.

The first unrest came in 1959 when the IOC held its session in Rome. Aleksei Romanov of the Soviet Union accused the South African NOC of "never having done anything to prevent apartheid," which was, he argued, an infringement of the Olympic rules. Reginald Honey of South Africa countered that he had a guarantee from his government that all South African athletes entered by their NOC for the Games were to be supplied with passports. Yet the following year when the Games were staged in Rome, the entire South African team was white.

In the following year South Africa became a republic and quickly strengthened its racial laws; some members of the IOC saw the plight of the country's nonwhite population getting worse. Their fears and worries were manifested in an offensive against South Africa by Andrianov of the USSR.

By 1963, at the IOC session in Baden-Baden, West Germany, the attitude had hardened and the IOC called upon the South African NOC to oppose publicly and in reality all racial discrimination in sport and competition. When the IOC met the following year at the Winter Games in Innsbruck, Austria, the members decided that this request had not been met and the invitation to compete in the Tokyo Summer Games was withdrawn. For South African athletes, white and nonwhite, the Olympic cord was cut. It is sad that South African children born after the 1960 Rome Games are now into the third decade of their lives and are still denied the opportunity of the Olympic experience, with all the incentive that means for schools, clubs, and international competition.

The IOC decision brought bitter resentment but undoubtedly motivated those outside sport who saw the perpetuation of apartheid as a compelling human problem. Politicians and governments used the Olympic platform to bring the South African problem to the attention of the world.

The Supreme Council for Sport in Africa (SCSA), comprised of African sports organisations, campaigned for South Africa's permanent expulsion from the Olympic Movement. There was considerable support from the Eastern European states and from groups within other countries, together with an organisation, based in London and consisting chiefly of expatriates, called the South African Non-Racial Olympic Committee. (Brundage insisted that it had no right to use the word "Olympic" in its title, which was therefore changed to "Open" to maintain the acronym SANROC.)

The IOC agreed at the meeting in Tehran, Iran, in 1967 to send a commission of enquiry to South Africa and Brundage invited me to be its chairman. I had been given my first office, that of *chef de protocole*, the previous year, but this was to be my first important undertaking for the Olympic Movement.

I told Brundage straightaway that I had doubts as to my suitability since I might be considered to have prejudged the situation through being a patron of the Irish Anti-Apartheid Society. Brundage decided that this was not a barrier. I therefore subsequently resigned from the anti-apartheid movement and reverted to the principle I had been taught to apply as a journalist: search for the facts and don't jump to conclusions beforehand.

On August 31, 1967, Brundage wrote me the following letter:

Thank you for all the copies of correspondence concerning the special commission to South Africa which you have sent to keep me advised on progress. I am glad to note that everything has finally been arranged and you are leaving next week. One last word before you depart.

If we are to judge apartheid *per se*, it is not for us to send a Commission at all. Our concern is with the NOC and what it is doing to comply with the Olympic regulations, especially Articles 24 and 25.

We had an analogous situation in 1936 when most of the

world condemned Nazism and many wanted to remove the Games from Berlin. So also, after the Second World War, many of those who were against Communism wanted to keep the Eastern countries out of the Games.

We must not become involved in political issues nor permit the Olympic Games to be used as a tool or as a weapon for an extraneous cause. Thank you for undertaking this delicate and important task. Please accept my best wishes for an interesting, successful and not too arduous commission.

Sincerely,

Avery Brundage

The important point is made in the second paragraph, where the question implied is: what has the South African NOC been doing to comply with Olympic regulations? From my personal experience, the answer is very little.

I fully concurred with Brundage's view that "we must not become involved in political issues nor let the Olympic Games be used as a tool or weapon for an extraneous cause." Yet when Brundage fought for the Games in Berlin, he was condemned as pro-Nazi. In my turn, in 1980 I was accused by the right of being pro-Communist over Moscow. This is far from the truth, as the Soviet authorities can attest.

The three-man commission consisted of myself and two African members, one white and one black. My black colleague was Sir Ade Ademola, a former chief justice of Nigeria, president of the Nigerian NOC, and a tower of strength in the Olympic Movement. If it had not been for constitutional changes in Nigeria, he would have been a local ruler. He was active in sport when at Cambridge and is one of the most cultured people I have ever met. The first black African member of the IOC, he was ideal to bridge the gulf in thought between the new, emerging world of his continent and the outside.

The white African member was Reginald Alexander, who had been mayor of Nairobi and a member of the legislative assembly when Kenya obtained its independence. Though as a white Kenyan he had survived difficult times, he regarded himself as an African quite as fully as any black. He had created an extremely good impression in the Olympic world by bringing black, European, and Indian Kenyans to the Olympic Games in the most integrated teams to come from any country. Extremely outspoken, he is an accountant by profession and is always delving for facts and figures.

We decided to assemble in Nairobi on September 6, 1967, and there we planned our method of working. Our brief was to report on facts and not to make any recommendations; and the report we produced was, as directed, not a general enquiry on apartheid but an enquiry into whether the South African NOC could and would conform to the IOC rules regarding discrimination in the Olympic Games against any person or country on the grounds of race, religion, or politics. The IOC rule is quite clear in referring to the Olympic Games and not to the politics of the country. However, the actions of governments can well affect the eligibility of an NOC, which must conform with Olympic principles and strive to be independent.

Although the trip confirmed my own worst fears about apartheid, we produced a very fair and balanced report from which an advocate for either side could quarry arguments to support his own case.

We arrived at Johannesburg on September 7, 1967, and were immediately informed that we were all staying at the same hotel, which, at that time, was a breakthrough; even VIPs, if nonwhite, were not previously permitted there. I was most anxious that we should not make any gaffes during our tour and I asked the liaison officer who was with us at the time whether there was anything special we should or should not do. He replied that we all had complete freedom of movement, but he did ask that if Ademola wished to relieve himself he should go up to his room and not use the public "Gents" cloakroom in the main part of the hotel! I replied that if this was so, he must put his request to Ademola himself. It was not my intention to instruct a former chief justice of Nigeria what to do in such a matter.

Our meetings got off to a bad start. Frank Braun, the chairman of the South African NOC, asked if they could have a representative at all times at the commission. In fact he had tried to preempt this question by announcing beforehand in the press that an NOC representative would be an observer at commission meetings. Such a move might have inhibited people from coming forward with evidence. Ademola was wholly opposed to the Braun suggestion and Alexander pointed out that the commission did not want anyone to be frightened. We tried to have it publicised as widely as possible that such a matter was for our discretion. What did come most firmly out of this initial meeting with the South African NOC officers was that they did not want us to have any contact with Denis Brutus, the leading member of SANROC, who was out of the country, not by his own choice. He had been the most active person in showing the world that under the existing arrangements South Africa could not conform to Olympic rules and principles. Certainly at that meeting it was confirmed that, under the existing laws, a non-white could not become a member of the South African NOC.

Confusion reigned. Many people who spoke to our commission came without proper briefing. Some of non-European stock were prepared to go along with the government attitude in return for sports facilities and competition—among their own group—but at the price that they did not have a voice or a vote in any matter.

E. Fyfe Sono, vice-president of the South African non-European athletic and cycling federation, said that if they continually made requests to the authorities they were branded as agitators. Yet they did so because, if there was to be parallel development, then the blacks, coloureds, and Indians should have the same facilities and opportunities as South African whites, which was not the case.

The view of the competitors came from Anne Fairlie, a South African swimmer who had broken two world records. She felt that the younger generation was prepared to integrate in sport. She said that in France black swimmers had competed against the South African team. "It really makes no difference at all," she said. A beautiful view, warped and distorted by a regime that wished to preserve its riches and feared for its future if anything but separate development was pursued.

We heard evidence from the various sporting bodies and were given the freedom to visit African townships, such as Soweto, as well as to interview people who were under house arrest or had restricted movement, besides those who had spent time as political prisoners on Robben Island.

After Johannesburg the commission visited Durban, East London, and Port Elizabeth and ended up in Cape Town, which is the most integrated, liberal, and tolerant place in South Africa. One hot day during the trip, Alexander decided to go for a swim and Ademola and I, walking along the seafront, sat down on a bench on the promenade for a rest. This action put us in breach of the law of the land, and we were told very rapidly by a plainclothes policeman that we could not sit on the bench together. There were benches for whites and benches for blacks. These incidents remain vividly in one's mind and make one realise how inhuman the whole system of separate development is.

When I was in Durban on September 11, a message was received that Prime Minister B. Vorster was anxious to see me next day. Accordingly, I flew back to Pretoria, where I saw him in his office together with R.W.J. Opperman, a member of the NOC executive board. Vorster had been interned during the war for being pro-German. He was dour but, I was assured, far more enlightened than many others in his cabinet. It was the minister in charge of sport, Frank Waring, of British stock, who seemed to be the most extreme and who, while the commission was actually in South Africa, made veiled threats that we deplored in our report. He said in a newspaper interview, "We are not going to have trials between whites and non-whites in South Africa." He said the country was not prepared to pay the price for mixed sport and that it would be impossible to find better sporting facilities for nonwhites anywhere in the world, which did make me wonder if he had travelled far.

I told the prime minister that we were trying to find ways of giving everybody an equal opportunity to compete in the Olympic Games but that, in view of South Africa's complete segregation in sport, it was impossible to make a fair selection either of teams or of individual competitors. He replied that selection could be made on the basis of statistics rather than competition. He was quite prepared to let a mixed team travel but would not allow the members to compete against each other at home, even in private, which made a mockery of the whole proposal.

I suggested that trials for the selection of Olympic candidates might be held outside South Africa, in countries where apartheid did not operate, if permission was given to potential competitors to leave. This Vorster also firmly ruled out. He could not agree to mixed trials outside South Africa and there could be no mixed trials in private within the country. He said South Africa was very anxious to compete in the Games but not if this meant integrated sport. He even took the question further by declaring that there could be no mixed teams in team sports. I found it a most depressing meeting. It underlined the isolation that South Africa was prepared to accept in order to preserve apartheid.

The prime minister and I made no headway and I rejoined the two other members of the commission, who had continued their investigations without me. It was apparent that the South Africans of European descent had every possible sporting facility, thanks to their money, their education, and their experience. The nonwhites were often well organised, but the facilities they had were clearly of a lower standard.

If the words of the prime minister and, to a greater extent, the minister of sport had given little hope, then an incident in Cape Town only made the three of us feel more depressed about the situation. When we arrived in Cape Town we were asked at a press conference whether we were going to an important rugby match at Newlands Park. I said the answer was no since we had so much work to do in a short period.

That evening a party was given for us at the Mount Nelson Hotel, where we were staying. It was mixed, which was very unusual. Several nonwhites said it was the first time they ever had been allowed into the hotel. During the party I received a message that someone from the Cape Province Rugby Football Union was anxious to see me outside.

The official brought an invitation to the rugby match, but clearly it was only for Alexander and myself. I went back to the party and told the liaison officer about this incident of discrimination against a member of our commission. I found it incredible that anyone could have acted in such a way, bearing in mind the nature of our task in South Africa. It helped to confirm my feeling that South Africa is a closed society and that many of its people do not comprehend the attitude of the rest of the world toward their apartheid policies.

When we were hearing evidence the following day I received a message that a deputation from the rugby union wanted to see us. Rugby is not an Olympic sport but, as we had a few minutes to spare, we agreed to meet them. Three men came into the room—the man who had offered the invitation the previous evening, another official of the rugby union, and Dr. Danie Craven, who has made genuine efforts to abolish apartheid in rugby. They had come to invite all three of us to the match. I told them we would let them know and, as soon as they had departed, I told my two colleagues that we must go to the game. Ademola objected, but only on the grounds that he did not like rugby—he was a soccer man. I told him the invitation was very important because this would be a unique occasion—a black African in the presidential box at Newlands Park, that sacrosanct stronghold of the Afrikaners, for whom rugby is a religion.

And so we went to the match. As we went up in the lift and eventually entered the president's room and stand, some European ladies moved away from us as if to avoid contamination. It was the strangest atmosphere I can ever remember. I have been in many odd situations in totalitarian countries, but this was eerier than anything else I have ever experienced. As soon as we entered the box, the photographers pounced for a picture of Ademola sitting among all those whites. The only other black spectators were behind the goalposts, in the worst possible position. It was an extremely good game, South African rugby at its best, and I enjoyed it hugely. At half time the press leaped over all the barriers and surrounded Ademola, asking him, "What do you think of the game?" His only comment was, "I prefer soccer," a classic reply on the part of the first black man to sit in the presidential box at Newlands Park.

In our report to the IOC we said that the government was strong and determined in its policy of separate development and, where necessary, imposed restrictions in sport by law. We found that the South African NOC had made serious, though unavailing, representations to the South African government, but took the view that it could not operate in open defiance of its government. The report was considered by the IOC at the session immediately prior to the 1968 Winter Games in Grenoble, France. It was not a well-attended meeting so the question of South Africa's position was settled by a postal vote. While our report fairly indicated that South Africa was not subscribing to Olympic rules and principles, the vote was in favour of keeping them in, provided their next team was multiracial with all their athletes enjoying equality of treatment. That, of course, could not be achieved in South Africa, but it could once they left for Mexico, where the Summer Games were to be held.

The door for South Africa's reentry to the Olympic arena, pushed open on what most people believed was an unhappy compromise, did not remain so long. The slim vote brought a predictable reaction from outside the Olympic Movement. Led by Abraham Ordia and Jean-Claude Ganga, the president and secretary-general of the SCSA, a campaign was mounted against the IOC. Soon there was a threat to boycott the Mexico Games. By April it appeared that forty countries, a large number of them from Eastern Europe and Africa, were prepared to withdraw if South Africa took part. Brundage was getting anxious messages from the Mexicans, who were clearly worried about the effect this was going to have on the celebration. Finally he called together his Executive Board for a meeting at the IOC headquarters in Lausanne in May.

Before arriving in Switzerland, Brundage slipped off for a four-day trip to South Africa, which seemed unnecessary after a commission had been sent less than twelve months before, particularly as he did not inform his Executive Board beforehand. His explanation was that he went to ask the South Africans to decline their invitation, but he did not get the answer for which he hoped. He flew back through the night, arriving at Geneva unshaven and looking very tired. Yet the man had enormous physical strength and, after a few hours' sleep, he called us together for a two-day debate on the subject.

I remember at this time looking out of the windows of the boardroom on the first floor, across to Lake Geneva, and seeing a magnolia tree in magnificent bloom. Its pastel colour and sheer beauty seemed utterly in contrast to the torment that was being suffered in that room. I noticed too, as time passed, a growing number of gentlemen lounging around in the sunshine on the lawn of the Château de Vidy. I recognised my own breed; they were journalists, and it dawned on me then that the IOC had not yet come to terms with the fact that the media of the world were now turning their focus more strongly than ever on the Olympic Movement, reporting on the Games and its troubles. That was to be borne out on the second day, when Brundage finally delivered our decision.

Much of the discussion concerned the belief that if a South African team went to Mexico there would be demonstrations against them; Brundage suggested that these might come from other than Mexicans. I felt at the time this was a spurious argument, an argument to help the IOC out of its predicament. My own view was that we should never have invited the South Africans in the first place.

The board agreed that because time was short, telegrams to all the IOC members should be sent calling for their support in withdrawing the South African invitation because of the international climate. There was no mention of danger to any team in Mexico because that discussion had angered General José Clark Flores, the former chairman of the Mexico City organising committee, who was on the Executive Board.

When Brundage met the press at an *ad hoc* conference on the garden steps of the headquarters, he was literally lifted off his feet as over 150 media representatives pressed around him. Within a few days the telex at the château had chattered out firm support for the somersault, with forty-seven members supporting the decision and sixteen against.

That outcome did not satisfy the opponents of apartheid, and African NOCs, backed by the SCSA and SANROC, maintained their call for expulsion. The door was finally closed on South Africa at Amsterdam in 1970.

The South Africans seemed to run out of patience at the Amsterdam IOC session. Whereas they had been eager to show respect for the Olympic Movement in all our past dealings, now there was a change. Ordia and Ganga, appearing as representatives of the NOCs of Nigeria and the Congo (Brazzaville), had prepared a statement in advance, but the South Africans hadn't, which was a break with custom. The South Africans were in constant telephone communication with their country right up to the day of the meeting, when Frank Braun made their presentation. Agitated, he lectured us, warning the IOC not to interfere in South African affairs. Even Ordia and Ganga were taken aback. The members of the IOC, particularly Brundage, did not take kindly to such behaviour, and the proposal to expel South Africa passed with a narrow majority.

It was a decision that had a profound effect on sport in South Africa and one that I regret. We did not have the machinery in our rules, as we do now, to suspend an NOC. This is what should have happened, because without any formal link it is difficult to get proper information about what is going on.

There was one human touch about this event that I think went unrecorded. Honey of South Africa, the oldest member of the IOC, elected in 1946, said that he would resign. There was no reason for him to do so; he had broken no rules or regulations and I felt we needed the link to South Africa that he could provide. So too did Ordia, and he sent a message asking the man who represented all that Ordia and his colleagues opposed to remain a member; Honey did so until his death in 1982 at the age of ninety-five.

While international sporting federations such as the soccer federation had already either suspended or expelled South Africa, our decision prompted the closure of more doors by other sports. That, in turn, brought changes in attitudes and there are now several sports with mixed events in South Africa. Track and field is one sport that has made progress, and around the country there are multiracial competitions. But, in the overall picture of South Africa, this is no more than window dressing.

Today there are those among the nonwhites who accept separate development and have their own associations and federations, receiving help from the government through its sports council. For these organisations good facilities have now been provided, but most nonwhites believe it is wrong to support them because they perpetrate apartheid. The thriving sports organisations are those that promote nonracial sport, and welcome white people to play with and against them. But without the benefit of government funds they often have to make do with facilities of a very poor standard.

After my election as president, *The Times* of London,

under the headline MR. BRUNDAGE MAKING HIS POSITION FELT, reported that when addressing a meeting of the Afrikaans press Brundage had said that South Africa should be readmitted to the Olympic Games, and undertook to do all he could to help achieve that end. The following year, when he attended the African Games in Lagos, he did not receive a great welcome and a seat had to be moved into the stand for him at the last moment.

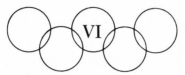

A Taste of Violence

After a boring flight to Mexico City for the 1968 Summer Games, I went straight to the Hotel Camino Real to catch up on lost sleep before a long round of meetings. I woke up to the sound of distant gunshots. A bloody battle was going on between the police and Army and thousands of students who had been attending a demonstration in the Square of the Three Cultures in a suburb of the city. In the months before the Games the authorities had grown more and more worried about student demonstrations, and only two weeks earlier there had been deaths in a smaller demonstration. Now here was another protest at the university campus opposite the main stadium.

Plainclothes police had taken over strategic flats in the square during the day and at a green Very flare they stormed the main balcony from which student leaders were making speeches. The square was then surrounded by troops and a battle raged for almost five hours. John Rodda of *The Guardian* reported that there were about ten thousand people in the square, one of the largest demonstrations there ever. He was held at gunpoint on the floor of the balcony, absolutely unable to know who was shooting at whom in the utter confusion. The Army fired bazooka shells into some of the nearby flats, while a marksman, perched high in a building overlooking the square, raked the balcony just above the heads of the student leaders, the bullets ricocheting about.

Not surprisingly, in a state of shock the following day,

Rodda sent in a note to the IOC session, to myself and Lord Exeter, asking that there be an independent IOC enquiry and suggesting that the Games be cancelled. Denis Howell, the British minister of sport, was dispatched from the Labour party conference at Blackpool by Harold Wilson, the prime minister, and many parents of European competitors were urging their children to return home.

The members of the IOC had been in complete ignorance of the situation before their arrival and many, like myself, regarded the Mexican demonstrations as having spread from Europe, where young Germans, French, and English had been on the streets, supporting differing causes, throughout the summer. But the situation in Mexico was different from that in Europe. The roots of discontent went deep into the country's history, and even on the routes to the Olympic sites the contrast between extreme wealth and extreme poverty was apparent.

The battle in the square ended the threat of disruption to the Games but at a high price in lives. The following day, with news of the shootings known around the world, the Mexican authorities announced that 35 had been killed and 100 injured, but other accounts indicated that these figures were a long way below the true ones. John Rodda, who had been in Mexico following the student demonstrations for ten days to investigate the background of the troubles, published figures on the victims gathered by the medical staffs of the city's hospitals, who were appalled at the carnage. Months later it was reported in the world press that at least 267 had been killed and 1,200 injured.

In fact, the battle in the Square of the Three Cultures had squeezed the very life not only out of its many victims but out of the spirit of the students. Brundage had warned the Mexican president, Gustavo Díaz Ordaz, that if there were demonstrations at the Olympic sites the Games would be cancelled; the government strategy in the square ensured that did not happen.

The one man who did not appear to be upset by what had occurred was General Clark of Mexico. He told his fellow IOC Executive Board members, when they met in agitated session next morning, that more people were killed in traffic accidents in Mexico every day than had been shot in the square that night, so what was all the fuss about? The Executive Board, still a gentlemanly body, would have liked to discuss the matter in the absence of Clark but could think of no way of politely excluding him—and he had no intention of tactfully offering to withdraw. I realised then that it might not be a good idea for any member actively involved in the organising of the Games to be serving at the same time on the Executive Board.

This was my first experience of violence at the Olympic Games and its sequel was exceptionally tight and oppressively visible security arrangements. The carrying of the Olympic torch to the top of the huge pyramid at Teotihuacán prior to the opening ceremony was, in itself, immensely dramatic. Yet for me it was marred by the armed guards who were stationed everywhere in full battle gear and with loaded rifles.

A major question was how President Díaz, who was due to open the Games, should be transported to the stadium, which was situated in the university grounds outside the city itself. A helicopter was considered but finally he went by car, setting out from his palace in the centre of Mexico City before the crowds had started to gather. The main thoroughfares were lined with armed soldiers and the areas surrounding the stadium were bristling with troops when we arrived in our bus.

Inside the main stadium at the opening ceremony, however, there was not a soldier to be seen, except those involved in the protocol. I am quite sure there were many armed plainclothes policemen, but the television pictures that went round the world of the first woman to bring the flame into an Olympic stadium, the doves, the colour of it all, and the cheering must have made some people wonder what all the fuss had been about.

The Games passed without further incident, except when three members of the Black Power movement gave the clenched-fist salute during the playing of the American national anthem. Demonstrations of a political nature are, of course, strictly banned, and the Black Power athletes were dealt with —severely and correctly in accordance with the rules—by the United States NOC.

There was also a more covert demonstration by the largely American crowd at the opening ceremony. It was shortly after suppression of the Dubcek experiment in Czechoslovakia and the Czech team received a standing ovation as it marched around the stadium—a spontaneous but cogent demonstration of the crowd's political support.

The riots in Mexico were, together with the tragic events at Munich in 1972, the most serious violent outbreaks connected with the Olympics during my involvement with the IOC; I discuss Munich more fully in a later chapter, for it does bear a chapter by itself.

Fortunately, security has its comic as well as its sad side, and I experienced my share of both, especially after my election as president when I was subject to very close personal protection almost everywhere except Britain and Ireland.

My first taste of police activity on my behalf came on September 11, 1972, when I flew from Munich to Geneva with Brundage in an executive jet. We arrived at the Château de Vidy to find groups of people, obviously plainclothes policemen, huddled together. I attempted to find out what had happened. It was only the next day that I discovered that a group of people had daubed the château with obscene graffiti, which had been scrubbed off by the police. Not a very polite welcome for the new president of the IOC.

Switzerland generally is not a good place to confront the law. However, even the Swiss can nod. On my way to the Dublin airport bound for Geneva, I heard on the car radio that very tight security checks were in operation at the Geneva airport because Arab-Israeli talks were taking place in the city. This I thought would delay my journey to Lausanne, but I was surprised and relieved to go through passport control without delay. Two days later I passed through passport control smoothly again on my way home. Before boarding the plane I decided to replace my Swiss money with English money and opened my wallet, which also contained my passport. Looking up at me was a picture of my wife. In my hurry to leave I had taken her passport instead of mine. A friend, George Bogle of the International Publishing Corporation, who had been with me during the war, happened to arrive at that moment. I told him what had happened and he asked what I was going to do. I said one thing was certain; I was not going back through the Swiss immigration authorities. We flew to London and, on arriving at Heathrow Airport, I went up to the most sympathetic-looking immigration officer I could find and explained that I had my wife's passport. He asked me where I had come from. "Switzerland," I said. "You cannot possibly have been in Switzerland on your wife's passport," he replied. "Any other country, but not there. They are so strict." I assured him I had and he looked at me in amazement. "Go on," he said pleasantly. "Get through as fast as you can."

Such a relaxed attitude was rare. More often I was subject to an excess of zeal on my behalf. On my way to a meeting of the Pan American Sports Organisation (PASO) in Santiago, Chile, at the end of May 1973, I stopped over in the charming, old-fashioned Uruguayan city of Montevideo. I stayed in a large suite in one of the city's most central hotels and on one occasion went out through one of the doors of my suite and later, on my return, tried to reenter it by another one around the corner. Half a dozen gentlemen were sitting on the floor playing cards and firmly barring my entry. They had been told to protect the president of the IOC but had no idea of what he looked like, and I, not speaking Spanish, was unable to enlighten them. There was no way I could get back into my suite until the management came to my rescue.

The following day I went shopping. The police were anxious to know exactly where I was going—something I did not know myself. By now I had an escort of some dozen plainclothesmen, but the shopping trip was a flop. A sudden inferiority complex overcame me when it came to going into shops and buying small souvenirs for half a dollar; I felt my escorts would be expecting the IOC president to be patronising at the Asprey or Hermés of Montevideo.

On my way from Montevideo to Santiago I had to pass through Argentina, where I was met at the Buenos Aires airport by Mario Negri, an IOC member and former president of the International Amateur Swimming Association (FINA), with officers of the Argentine NOC. I was given the VIP treatment: my passport was taken from me to avoid queuing formalities, while my luggage had been booked through. There was quite a lot of shooting in the city that day and I felt that my Argentine friends might wish to get home as early as possible. I told them not to await my departure and my passport was duly returned. Later on I was ordered to pass through emigration but was told I could not leave the country. "Why?" I asked. "Because you have not arrived," I was told. My passport had not been stamped on entry. I was obviously physically visible but the plane was delayed for at least an hour to find a higher official to stamp my passport to show I had passed through immigration that morning before emigrating that evening.

Another security problem with an amusing aspect occurred the following year when, at the invitation of Sir Stanley Rous, the outgoing president of the International Association Football (soccer) Federation (FIFA), I returned to the Munich Stadium for the first time since the tragic 1972 Games there for the finals of the World Cup between Germany and Holland. U.S. Secretary of State Henry Kissinger, who was born near Munich and is a keen sportsman, had decided at the last moment to attend. This unexpected request was an embarrassment, both to the organisers and to the German government. While it was possible to place Kissinger and, perhaps, one secretary or aide in the presidential box, American secretaries of state do not travel alone. In addition to his officials he had a large number of his own security men. The German authorities had to go out on the streets to buy black market tickets for all these officials to watch the match.

As I arrived at the room we used for refreshments, behind the presidential stand, I was conscious of several people arguing. The argument was between the German plainclothes police and Kissinger's personal bodyguards, who were claiming it was their duty to be in the box as close as possible to Kissinger. The German argument, naturally, was that Kissinger was in Germany and accordingly his protection was their responsibility. I had a feeling that possibly the real question at issue was which lot of security men should be in the box to see the game. In the end I think they split the difference. At all events we sat surrounded by German plainclothesmen on one side and American agents with their radio sets (which looked like hearing aids) and guns on the other.

The horror of the assassinations in the Olympic Village in Munich changed the whole concept of security, which as a result took a very high priority in the Montreal Games in 1976. In Canada, as in many federal states, there are several police forces: There is the federal force, the Royal Canadian Mounted Police, a force for each province, and a force for each city. As the Games were to be held in Montreal, it was the Montreal city police who were in charge of security, and it appeared they were going to be very heavy-handed and in all ways the reverse of the Germans in Munich.

At all times in Montreal I had three policemen with me— one from the city of Montreal, one from the Royal Canadian Mounted Police, and one from the Quebec police—except when I went into Ontario, where the latter two handed me over at the border. Members of the Canadian Artillery, who were mostly used to crown caps, became dab hands at uncorking wine bottles, one of them having opened one for my wife with his bayonet. Altogether, they were most helpful and kind and have been friends with us ever since, as have the members of the state police and federal agents who looked after me at Lake Placid.

At the Prague IOC session in 1977, shortly after I had had a coronary, I was taking a lot of exercise. The Czech organisers told me that if I was going out I should advise the police, who would look after me, but unfortunately the Prague policemen were rather large and obviously did most of their policing from the seat of a car. There were sad faces when they found I was leading them on brisk walks through the city, and even sadder when I took them to mass in the cathedral on Sunday, in company with my colleague and later successor, Juan Antonio Samaranch. They had to stand to attention while we sat in our special pew for one of the longest religious ceremonies I have experienced since the reforms of Vatican II.

By contrast, when I went to mass in the Olympic Village in Moscow, I found I was being asked by my Soviet colleagues at the last moment for a lift in the same direction. They would often come to mass, which took place in a church organised on an ecumenical basis, with an Austrian priest, the representative of the pope, and a French-speaking Lithuanian priest jointly in charge. Several services for different denominations used to take place concurrently in this special chapel. No doubt some of my Marxist-Leninist friends were interested to see in action what they believed was mumbo jumbo. But some of them were also impressed to find so many young athletes attending these services.

If I appear frivolous about some of my security experience, it is not really funny: it is an ever increasing problem facing the Olympic Games and international sport. In this mad world the incidents of violence at Mexico and Munich, and throughout many areas of society, made security a price that had to be paid for the Games to continue. It is an area in which sophistication must be pursued, probably at high cost, in order that the world's sportsmen may concentrate upon their competition in peace of mind.

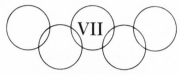

President-Elect

When I was elected president of the IOC in Munich in 1972, I recalled my conversation with Arthur MacWeeney twenty years before. In 1952 the sportswriter said to me in Helsinki, "Michael, I see no reason why you should not one day be president of the IOC." I asked him why he thought so. I have never forgotten his reply: "Because Mr. Brundage comes from a very large country and must be fettered with its politics. Surely it would be better for the president of an international body such as the IOC to come from a small country."

At the time I shrugged off the idea as a joke, pointing out that I could not afford to serve in the post; nor, at that moment, had I the time or the desire and ambition. But as the years went by and my Olympic career began to develop, I kept thinking of MacWeeney's prophecy. While I never pursued the post, the stepping-stones within the Olympic Movement, and particularly the IOC, seemed laid out before me to that end, and that "little country" theory of MacWeeney's seemed more and more vital as sport and the Olympic Games moved deeper into the political jungle.

My first post was that of *chef de protocole*. I was elected to the post in Rome in 1966. This carried little executive power but did ensure that I was constantly in touch with the members during the sessions. In those days the IOC was much more of a club than it is today and the annual session was a gathering of friends that formed groups whose common denominator was language or political and geographical location. Thus it would be possible to go from one session to another and not to get to know many members. Yet as *chef de protocole*, I had an introduction to every member, since it was my task to ensure that members and their wives sat in their proper seats, were on time for all the official functions, and were in the correct order for meeting heads of state. Thus it provided a means of introduction, so that I came to know more about all the members and they came to know something of me. It may sound a simple matter, yet, when I look back, I really believe it was of far more value than all the canvassing and lobbying that went on for various IOC posts at that time.

In 1967 I stood for a single vacancy on the Executive Board and was elected without opposition. Two years later I was appointed chairman of the Press Committee (later called the Press Commission), which meant I presided over or attended press conferences. This brought me publicity—there was now another "Olympic" face besides that of Brundage. Also, because of my newspaper background, I understood what journalists required, and as I made their lives a little easier and brought some clarity out of the mystery of the way the Olympic Movement worked, I gained respect.

One of my jobs at the Rome session as *chef de protocole* had been to stop the leaks of information that were coming out of the session as members wandered out of the conference room and talked to journalists. *L'Équipe*, the French newspaper, at one time was so well informed it seemed to have a reporter in the session. Brundage agreed that to quell this flow I should have the key of the conference hall and we should all be locked in. Members, of course, with a discreet nod were allowed out, but there were one or two weak-bladdered members about whom I remained suspicious, and at the end none were allowed out until the votes had been counted and announced for the Games of 1972.

The two key appointments on the road to the presidential chair have been *chef de protocole* and chairman of the Press Commission. It is, I feel, not without coincidence that the current president followed me in these two positions before he was elected to lead the movement in 1980. He still retains his place as chairman of the Press Commission, which confirms my belief that this is one of our most important working groups.

It was in 1968 at the session preceding the Mexico Games that I was elected vice-president. I was in fact asked by many members to stand for the presidency. I explained that I could not take on the task until such time as the IOC allowed its president an expense account. I felt I could not bear the cost and did not think that the president should be expected to do so; more important, I was unwilling to oppose Brundage if he wished to stand yet again, as he did. This did not prevent him from coming to me in some agitation to ask me whether I intended to run or not. He said people had told him that he would get most of the votes. I assured him that I was not standing but that people had told me I would get most of the votes if I did. Obviously many members of the IOC were anxious to keep in with both sides; such are the cynical ways of this "gentlemen's club." I was, however, elected a vice-president, defeating the only other contender on that occasion, the senior French member, Jean, Count de Beaumont, who won a place on the Executive Board.

All this gave me the feeling that the IOC wanted me as its president and there appeared to be no other rising contender. In the following years I found that more and more of the English-speaking media were campaigning for me.

The next presidential election occurred at the Munich Games IOC session of 1972 against a background of manoeuvring and restlessness, which had already lasted several years. The cause of this was the character of my predecessor—his rocklike conservatism, strong prejudices, and spirit of tough independence. Born in Detroit in 1887, he made his fortune early in life, which gave him advantages when it came to travel and taking time off from business. But he was not originally rich. In later years he would recall with pride how, as a young athlete, he had travelled to the Games in Stockholm in 1912 without asking for financial assistance from anybody. He was intransigent on the question of amateurism in sport, and unable to accept any progress in this matter to meet the conditions of modern times. He hated the Winter Games, with their overtones of professionalism and advertising, and was delighted when things began to go wrong in Denver in 1976.

One of his interests was Oriental art, for which he acquired a liking after paying a visit to the Chinese Exhibition in London in 1936. He went to Shanghai before the war, but after the revolution there was not allowed on the mainland, though he was welcome in Taipei. This did not help when it came to the difficulties involved in the admission of mainland China to the Olympic Movement, as he was considered to support Washington's recognition of the Nationalist government in Taiwan as the government of China.

After his death in 1975, a strange part of Brundage's background came to light. Though a married man, he had had two children by a Finnish woman who lived on the west coast of the United States, where Brundage had a home.

At the height of the Moscow boycott crisis I received a distraught letter from Douglas Roby, a member of the IOC for the United States, saying that nothing that was going on at that time could be as bad as the "terrible scandal" about to break regarding Brundage. Personally I thought it showed a pleasantly human side to the man. The first Mrs. Brundage (he remarried after his retirement), who was three years younger than her husband, although most members thought she was older, was a distinguished lady, admired by all when she attended IOC sessions before failing health prevented her accompanying Brundage. It was known by many members that there were other women in Brundage's life. In this respect his vitality amazed many of his colleagues, for often after a long day's work he would dance until the early hours—even when he was in his eighties. The "scandal" did not break until after the Moscow Games and, in an application against the Brundage estate, it was revealed that Brundage had tried to ensure when the children were born that no revelation would be made.

Brundage was always very kind and would help anyone who needed it, but he was very suspicious of possible rivals. During the Second World War he was prominent in the campaign to keep the United States out of the conflict and that made him unpopular. He was not a person to fall out with, yet his loyalty to those whom he trusted was exemplary and never wavered. He was touchy about his authority and his vanity was considerable. It may sound uncharitable, but if he had not seen

trouble ahead for Montreal it would have been difficult to dis-
lodge him from the presidency in 1972. As it was, he contented
himself with telling me, with much relish, that the Montreal
Games would never take place.

He was paternalistic, and disliked the near democracy of
the Olympic congresses (joint meetings of the IOC, NOCs, IFs,
and invited interested parties), which he opposed holding until
eventually overruled by the Executive Board and the members.
All the IOC sessions are held in private and the only open
channel to the NOCs and IFs was through separate meetings
with the Executive Board of the IOC. Congresses are open
forums where you can put your finger on the pulse of events and
see the manner in which fashions and ideas are changing. It is
impossible to do that in this day and age behind the closed doors
of the IOC session, although I still believe that this is the way
the IOC should conduct its business as people tend to make political speeches in public and say something nearer the truth in
private.

Brundage, too, had the habit, rather like certain popes, of
trotting out a few foreign phrases in an appalling accent for the
benefit of his audiences from different countries, unaware that
many of us found this embarrassing and patronising. He was
emotional, even sentimental, and broke down and cried at a
dinner given to mark his retirement by the international federations at the Lausanne Palace Hotel.

His autocratic ways in running the Olympic Movement
were very different from my own. Once, at a 1969 Executive
Board meeting in Warsaw, I lost my temper, banged the table,
and called him a Fascist. This only confirmed his suspicion that
I was a "goddamn subversive."

Yet, when all these criticisms have been made, his contribution to the Olympic Movement was immense. If he had not
succeeded to the presidency at Helsinki in 1952, the Olympic
Movement might well have collapsed under the strains of postwar disruption and disorganisation. It needed a firm hand to get
things moving. His attitude of allegiance to the Olympic principles welded together the greater part of the world under the
Olympic flag and this contribution must never be forgotten;
what will be remembered, however, is that he went on too long,

shackled to rules and ideas that, to the youth of the world, were outdated and, to their seniors, largely unworkable. On reflection, he probably left four years too late.

Brundage was first nominated as president of the IOC by outgoing President Edström at Helsinki in 1952. He defeated Lord Exeter, who twelve years later in Tokyo challenged Brundage again, as criticism of the latter's intransigence first began to surface. Because it was known that attendance at the session would be small, there was a postal vote—the one and only time that this has happened in an election for the IOC presidency. Brundage won again. Some members had felt that Exeter should have resigned as president of the International Amateur Athletic Federation before standing again for the presidency of the IOC. Then too, better the devil you know. Though Brundage's autocratic attitude made him enemies, he commanded respect and was not disliked by the IOC as a whole.

I think it was a great pity that Exeter lost in 1964. At fifty-nine, which he was then, he could have given invaluable service to the IOC over the next eight to twelve years. His knowledge both of track and field and of the Olympic Movement was immense. World famous as a hurdler and as a gold and silver Olympic medallist, he had been a member of the IOC since 1936, a vice-president and several times a member of the Executive Board. He had brilliantly organised the 1948 Games in London. Had Exeter defeated Brundage I would not have been president, for there would have been no question of yet another English-speaker following on so soon. But I am still sorry he lost.

Count de Beaumont was the next man to oppose Brundage, in 1968. Stylish, generous, and kind, Beaumont also had the resources of a large bank, the Banque Rivaud, behind him, and put his financial expertise unstintingly at the movement's disposal. He was a pioneer of Olympic Solidarity, which gives financial support to the less affluent NOCs, and was one of the first to suggest the IOC Press Commission. As a sportsman in his prime he was one of the best shots in the world.

However, he also lost to Brundage. Beaumont was a weaker candidate and members were resigned not to upset the status quo under these circumstances.

But by the time of the Munich Games in 1972, the situation

had changed. First, Brundage had announced his willingness to retire. Second, the financial position of the IOC, thanks to advances on television rights for the forthcoming Games, had considerably improved. So when I was once more approached to let my name go forward, I could agree in the knowledge that I would not be opposing a president who greatly desired to stay on. I could also stipulate that I would need payment of bare expenses.

Brundage openly boasted that it cost him $75,000 a year to be president of the IOC. I reckoned I could match him in devotion but not in cash, and made it clear from the start that I would not allow my name to go forward unless my basic expenses—travelling, telephone, postage, secretarial services, and so forth—could be guaranteed. I was fortunate in having a number of independent directorships in companies rather than a nine-to-five job. I would therefore be in a position to give to my IOC duties as much time as they required, and hoped that, with careful planning, I would be able to continue my normal family and business life as well.

The lobbying, canvassing, and whispering that go on at the time of elections for the IOC presidency are totally inappropriate in such a body. However, in 1972 my own position as a candidate was strengthened by the lobbying of the English-speaking press. By the time of the Munich session I was senior vice-president. I knew there was strong support for me among the members and I was sure that I would win the vote when a matter of protocol relating to the election was discussed. I had said that I would stand for an eight-year period, which is laid down in the rules, but there was discussion as to whether this should be reduced to four years, a term that Beaumont, who was running against me, preferred. There was a straw poll and the eight-year term was heavily favoured.

At the time of the vote, Beaumont and I stood outside the conference room, and when the decision had been reached Brundage came out with the other members and we walked to the top of the stairs of the town hall, where the meeting was held. By then the nods and winks I saw indicated that I had won, but the official announcement came from Brundage. As is often the case in such circumstances the achievement, if that is what it was, came as something of an anticlimax. I was delighted, of course, but felt the sting of defeat that my opponent, a noble man in every sense of the word, was bearing. He was to become a very close colleague, wise and loyal and particularly helpful in matters of finance.

It was warm and sunny when I returned for the luncheon break to the Hotel Vierjahrzeiten, where my wife was waiting in the bar. She stood up, spread open her arms, and greeted me, *"Monsieur le Président,"* which expressed, I felt, our affection for French, the first language of the Olympic Movement. In most of my twenty years as a member my wife had been too busy raising our four children, or had been in too poor health, to attend many of the sessions with me. But now she was the president's lady and could look forward, I hoped, to travel and splendid occasions. Little did I realise then the burdens that lay ahead.

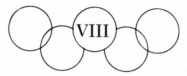

Massacre at Munich

W orn and weary, IOC member Willi Daume of West Germany, who had been instrumental in bringing the 1972 Summer Games to Munich, walked into the conference room of the Hotel Vierjahrzeiten where the IOC was in session and, with a smile of relief, announced that the Israeli hostages were safe. The members applauded and, although it was nearly eleven at night, we carried on with the business on the agenda until past midnight. Amid the confusion, anguish, and sadness of the Munich Games, blackened in the cause of Palestinian terrorism, this was the most twisted hour of all. At the time we were concerning ourselves with Olympic business, ten young Israelis were dying at Fürstenfeldbruck air base. We went to our beds ignorant of these events and while we slept the world learned the truth.

Taking the Games back to Germany in 1972, to the place where Nazism had festered, was an event of immense world significance. It was intended to show the world that Germany had risen from the ashes of war and that its youth could take part in wholesome sporting competitions. Instead, what the world saw was a brutal and horrifying massacre.

My first knowledge of Munich came from my work as a diplomatic writer before the Second World War. With other journalists I edited *Four Days,* a chronicle of the Munich crisis talks in 1938, seen through the eyes of a group of reporters from many parts of the world. The first time I actually visited Munich was shortly after the war. I decided to go on to Innsbruck and asked my driver, who was from Berlin, whether we would pass Dachau. He denied any knowledge of such a place—which, by 1972, would become a centre of pilgrimage to remind the Germans of their guilt, for it was but a few miles away from another anti-Semitic act of murder, in Munich.

On September 4, 1972, I went to Kiel, a thousand kilometres from Munich, to watch the sailing events. Early the following morning we boarded the yacht *Germania VI* of West German IOC member Berthold Beitz (head of the Krupp organisation), and set off on a sunny morning out into the Baltic to watch the day's races. Suddenly an official launch raced up alongside us and we were told what had happened in Munich.

Eight Palestinian terrorists had stormed their way into the Israeli quarters in the Olympic Village in the early hours of September 5. They took nine athletes and two of their bodyguards hostage. One Israeli was killed in the initial attack and the remaining ten perished, with five terrorists, soon after midnight. It was a time of nightmare and confusion. The Games went on but the world now had to recognise that hatred and prejudice were still a part of human affairs.

There have been many analyses of events to discover whether another course of action, or rather response, might have brought a happier outcome. But it is important to remember that the raid on the Munich Village was, in fact, one of the first acts of this kind on such a scale.

Meanwhile Brundage had been woken with the news of the attack at about five in the morning and set off from his hotel, without leaving any word or message to the IOC or its officials as to what had occurred or where he was going. He stayed in the Village all day and eventually attached himself to the *Krisenstab* (crises group), which included the head of the Munich police and Hans-Dietrich Genscher, then West German minister of the interior (who later as foreign minister was among those responsible for the German government's decision not to go to Moscow). Brundage emphasized the need to get the terrorists and their hostages off Olympic territory. That, of course, might have been a good strategy but the world has learned through subsequent such ordeals that time is the factor that erodes the resistance and resolve of many terrorists.

We sped back to shore after the alarm and prepared to return to Munich, only to find another message awaiting us, this one from Brundage saying that it was not necessary for us to return. We ignored Brundage's cable and returned from Kiel in a Krupp company plane, arriving at the hotel at about six P.M. Throughout the day in Munich members had been trying to get in touch with Brundage to call a meeting. Maurice Herzog of France had gone to the Village to get enough signatures to call a session—although, in point of fact, the IOC is in session until the Games end.

Beaumont and I were particularly upset by Brundage's seemingly insane attempt to deal with the whole situation himself. I took care in due course to see that a record appeared in the minutes of both the visit to Kiel of myself and my colleagues and of the countermanding telegram. The site of the Games is, in theory, Olympic territory, but this was a crisis far beyond the scope of the IOC. The members of the IOC felt that the president should have lost no time in calling in the organising committee and the federal German and Bavarian governments.

I immediately called an Executive Board meeting, which assembled at about seven P.M. without Brundage. The board decided to call a full IOC session at ten that night. When Brundage eventually returned to the hotel and joined the board at about seven-thirty P.M. he looked drawn and anxious. He was against the board's unanimous decision to call the session of the IOC and still seemed determined to do everything himself. He explained to the board what had happened and gave details, as far as he knew, of the attack by the Black September terrorists early that morning. He said he had proceeded alone to the Village two and a half hours later and had spent the day there. He read out to us the terms of a terrorist's ultimatum for the release of 256 Palestinian prisoners held in Israeli jails, in return for the release of the hostage Israeli athletes. It was quite evident that the demands called for decisions at the international political level. The difficulty was that the terrorists had begun by giving their opponents only a few hours in which to act. We also learned they continued to demand the release of the political prisoners in Israel or a further hostage would be killed every hour. There was frantic international telephoning between Munich, Bonn, Tel Aviv, Cairo, and Tunis, the key cities in which decisions might be made by German, Arab, or Israeli governments. The German authorities were doing all they could to ensure that there would be no further bloodshed and that the hostages would be released. The Arab governments suggested the hostages and the Black September gang might be taken to Egypt.

The German authorities, both federal and Bavarian state, were informed by Israeli ambassador Ben Horin, acting on the instructions of Prime Minister Golda Meir, who was personally handling the incident, that the government in Israel would in no way modify its decision not to release any of the political prisoners it was holding. However, the Israelis did display interest in the Egyptian plan, subject to various conditions.

It is recorded by Serge Groussard, who has written the most detailed account of these events in *The Blood of Israel* (New York: William Morrow and Company, 1975), that Chancellor Willi Brandt was very disappointed by the inflexibility of the Israeli position, but it was decided not to accede to the fedayeen's demands.

Brundage informed the Executive Board that he had announced at three-thirty in the afternoon that the Games would be postponed until the following day, calling for a memorial service for the two hostages who had died in the initial raid. Next he brought IOC member Ahmed Touny of Egypt to meet the chief of the German police and the mayor of the Village, Walter Tröger, later secretary-general of the West German NOC, and among them it was arranged that he should act as intermediary with the terrorists. On the authority of the organising committee, he offered a guarantee of safe conduct out of the country and whatever sum of money they asked in return for the release of the hostages.

This offer was refused. The terrorists repeated their demand for the release of the prisoners and made clear that they were fully prepared to sacrifice their own lives. The only concession Touny could bring back was an extension of the time limit by one hour.

The possibility of an attack on the house was discussed but rejected on the grounds that the risk of opening fire in a confined space on a group of obviously well-trained professionals was too great. It was therefore decided to fly captors and captives to Fürstenfeldbruck flying field and try to pick off the fedayeen with special snipers at the airfield.

All this and much more happened in the space of twenty-four hours, with the IOC members going to their beds mourning the loss of two Israelis, yet relieved, wrongly, at the supposed rescue of the remainder, as Daume had inadvertently misinformed us.

Newsmen at the darkened airport, though, were hearing different stories and the sight of a burning helicopter and more shooting led to rumour and counterrumour. Finally, the West German officials went to the Olympic Press Centre at three in the morning on September 6 and made the facts of the massacre known. Even so, the world's press was angered by the insistence of the spokesman on going through the entire day's events in a forty-five-minute speech before telling the newsmen what they wanted to know: "Are they dead or alive?"

We were informed of the final tragedy individually or by radio early in the morning; the German effort to save the hostages had ended in their deaths amid the chaos of the airfield. The Executive Board reassembled with a new and difficult question to resolve: should the Games continue?

The situation was extremely delicate. We had heard earlier that the Dutch team, for example, was under pressure to return home immediately, while certain of the Arab countries were considering withdrawing, or had already withdrawn, in the interest of their own safety. The decision—to cancel or not—was a hard one to make, but I believe that Brundage was right to continue and that his stubborn determination saved the Olympic Movement one last time. My own feeling coincided with his and in a way was a gut reaction: I was convinced that to cancel the Games in this tense moment would only bring further troubles. It would be impossible to evacuate all the competitors, officials, and spectators rapidly from Munich and there would inevitably be demonstrations. I had in mind the scenes in Dublin that had followed Bloody Sunday in Londonderry, Northern Ireland, when the British forces fired on marchers, earlier in the year. I had watched them on television during the Winter Games in Sapporo, Japan, and had seen how people who had nothing to do, because of the day of mourning that had been declared, roamed around the city and finally set fire to the British embassy. It is essential at such moments of crisis to keep people occupied. The art of the politician when things are going wrong is to find something for the populace to do.

At the board meeting reconvened on the morning of September 6, Brundage explained the various courses open. Then the organising committee announced a service of mourning at ten A.M. that day. Events that had been cancelled the day before would be held in the afternoon and there would be further small readjustments for logistic reasons connected, for instance, with the presale of tickets. Such matters may seem trivial under the circumstances but were of great importance from the administrative point of view. The West Germans had the stadium prepared in time for the service and we proceeded directly to it from the meeting. The Munich Opera House orchestra began a mourning service with Beethoven's *Egmont* Overture. Unfortunately, however, Brundage chose this occasion to commit another gaffe. Standing in the centre of the arena to pay his tribute to the dead, he decided for some reason to make a pointed reference to the African countries that had threatened to withdraw from the Games if the Rhodesian team took part.

As he spoke, I could sense the wrath not merely of the Africans but of the spectators and IOC members of all sorts. I remonstrated with him immediately after he returned to the box, deploring his speech and regretting his insensitivity, which indeed I found truly amazing and out of character; and no sooner had we arrived back at the hotel than representatives gathered from the African countries, led by Ordia and Ganga of the SCSA.

It was not what he said that was objectionable in itself, but the occasion on which he said it. He himself was quite adamant that he had said nothing out of place, but the Executive Board members were unanimous in considering him at fault. We agreed that he had introduced into a solemn memorial service something of a highly political nature, quite unconnected with the circumstances of the present tragedy. We therefore summoned, for the same afternoon, a meeting of the board. Brundage opened the meeting by reading a statement that ran:

The reference to Rhodesia in my remarks this morning was deliberate. It was intended to fortify the African sports leaders in their efforts to become free from their political masters. The reactions to the Rhodesian decision in mail and cables and the press of the world is about 500–1 against the political intrusion into the sports world, and the African politicians should know it. You will remember this sentence solicited the most applause from the spectators of the morning. There was no intention to tie this with the criminal terrorist action.

This exceptionally naïve statement merely added fuel to the flames. Both my Soviet colleague Andrianov and I felt particularly strongly that the president's speech further alienated the African countries, which were known to be holding a special meeting that evening to discuss the matter. We had enough problems on our hands without this one being added, and it was agreed that Arthur Takac, the IOC's technical director, should attend the meeting of the African countries and tell them that the president would be willing to speak to them and clarify his statement if they so wished. I knew quite well, however, that they would find this unacceptable as Brundage was completely *persona non grata* with all the African states.

We met again next morning, September 7, when Herman van Karnebeek reported further trouble in Holland and further demands for the Dutch team to withdraw. President Gustav Heinemann of West Germany had made a carefully worded speech at the memorial service and this had been discussed by the Dutch team members, who had decided to continue competing. They considered, however, that there should be no receptions, music, or such like, and that the closing ceremony should be abbreviated. This was the view of all of us. The Executive Board of the IOC then made the following announcement: "The Olympic Games are proceeding for the sake of sport and sport only. All official receptions are cancelled. All ceremonies will be kept as simple as possible."

At last, after much pressure, Brundage was persuaded that he had erred and he issued a personal statement, which read: "As President of the International Olympic Committee we regret any misinterpretation of the remarks made during the solemn memorial service in the stadium yesterday. There was not the slightest intention of linking the Rhodesia question, which was purely a matter of sport, with an act of terrorism universally condemned." And that was the end of that.

It was perhaps ironic that poor Brundage, who thought he had already said farewell to the presidency and only expected to preside over an Executive Board meeting, should have found himself in this predicament. But I felt more sorry for Willi Daume and my other German colleagues, including members of the federal and Bavarian governments and my friend Hans-Jochen Vogel, the mayor of Munich up to 1972, later minister of justice in the government of Helmut Schmidt, mayor of Berlin, and leader of West Germany's Social Democratic party. All were liberal-minded sportsmen who were doing their best to organise Games worthy of their country and to show that sport can unite the world.

The terrorists' attack negated all their goodwill with the most brutal use of sport for political ends. A Palestinian interviewed by Christopher Dobson and Ronald Payne when they were researching their book on terrorism, *The Carlos Complex*, proudly declared: "We recognize that sport is the modern religion of the western world ... so we decided to use the Olympics, the most sacred ceremony of this religion, to make the world pay attention to us." The world did, but with fateful consequences for those who had planned the attack.

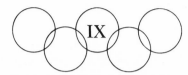

UNESCO and the Third World

The power of the International Olympic Committee rests in its autonomy. As a trusteeship it is answerable to none, yet in the complex, fast-moving modern world it needs to perform deft sidesteps to avoid those who would use it for their own ends. Only a structure that can provide swift and positive action is able to thus counteract danger. One such threat to the IOC's existence came in 1977 and 1978.

The United Nations Educational, Scientific, and Cultural Organisation (UNESCO) suddenly wanted not only to play a role in sports education, which was its responsibility, but to control, organise, and administer all sport. Some representatives wanted to run both the international federations and the Olympic Games.

I first became aware of UNESCO's sporting potential, either for good or ill, in 1973 when I met the director general, René Maheu, at the African Games in Lagos. This Frenchman was interested in sport and anxious to play a full part in its promotion through UNESCO. My previous experience with UNESCO, on its cultural side during the International Art Critics' Association Congress in Dublin in 1953, had left me extremely cynical about it; it struck me as a very good shelter for superfluous civil servants and unwanted diplomats, and its massive international bureaucracy provides a perfect demonstration of the operation of Parkinson's law. Its work in certain spheres, such as the restoration of national and international monuments, is of the most professional nature, as are many of its cultural activities. But its heavy involvement with the media in the reporting of events in the Third World is controversial. It must have a responsibility in the field of education in sport, yet this side of its work was completely undeveloped until some of its members woke up to the fact and went too far the other way.

As a result of these contacts I agreed to meet the new director general; Dr. Amadou-Mahtar M'Bow of Senegal, and to address a meeting of UNESCO in Paris in April 1977.

In the months before this speech I was getting indications that the idea of an Olympic takeover was being seriously mooted in the corridors of UNESCO power. Thus I decided in the most succinct manner possible to point out the independence of sport and its administration by explaining the structure of the IOC, outlining the changes in social and economic climate since 1894 when Coubertin called for the revival of the Games in the city where I was addressing the members of UNESCO. I also tackled what I thought was the role UNESCO should play. I said:

Gone are the days when a concrete schoolyard was sufficient for recreation. You, gentlemen, are closely associated with this.

The ideal would be for no future schools to be built in either the public or private sector without adequate facilities for recreation, nor should there be urban or rural development without this in mind. The facilities will vary in different parts of the world, depending on the climate, local sporting traditions, wealth, and political divisions. It is on this basis that the sportsmen or -women of the future evolve. Only a few will reach the Olympic Games but, inspired by the high-performance competitors, they will endeavour to emulate them. . . .

The view of the IOC is that it wishes the greatest support and assistance from the government authorities for the development of sport through NOCs. It is natural and correct that if governments give finance, they must insist it is correctly spent. We do ask that sport should not be a shuttlecock of national politics and that all NOCs must have freedom of action, not to be dictated to by political considerations or control, which would endanger the freedom of the individual or sport. We all aspire to promote this, whatever our political philosophies. It is for this

basic reason I am here today to assure you of our closest cooperation and also to express our pleasure that UNESCO has now taken the initiative in assisting in developing sport.

I hoped that this would disarm the illusionists around me, but I knew that part of the attack had come from the very determined Soviet delegates, who were talking about so-called democratisation of the Olympic Movement. In any case, this was the beginning of a very important dialogue between the Olympic Movement and UNESCO.

It was necessary to establish clearly and quickly the position of the IOC and the sporting federations. This was achieved through the Tripartite Commission, a group comprised of IOC members and representatives of the NOCs and International Federations, which had been created to prepare for the congress in Varna, Bulgaria, in 1973 but which I retained because of its usefulness in bringing together the views of the various organisations. I was criticised by some IOC members for preserving this umbrella group, since they thought it might usurp the IOC's paramount authority.

Thus when I called the Tripartite Commission to look at the UNESCO problem and prepare a manifesto, some IOC members said that the commission had exceeded its authority, which really meant I had stepped out of line since I was its chairman. My response to them was that if we had not acted rapidly but waited for a general session of the IOC among some seventy or eighty members, then we would have lost the initiative. The manifesto succeeded, although it was described in the press as an attack by the free, nongovernmental bodies on UNESCO. In point of fact it cleared the air, stating where each one's responsibility lay.

UNESCO was upset by being singled out in the following paragraph: "The national and international organisations responsible for sport have now become aware of the traditions and decisions of governmental or non-governmental agencies like UNESCO. They welcome the educational aspect of the action of public authorities but they warn the great mass of sportsmen against certain aspects of interference that risk diverting sport from its true purpose." It is now quite clear where the responsibilities of the IOC, the IFs, and the NOCs rest, and also those of UNESCO, its duties being more in education.

I also attended a conference of Western European ministers in Paris and again reiterated the need for freedom of sport from politics. I have always been very well supported by the majority of Western sports ministers, especially those of Britain, Ireland, and West Germany. They had no desire to interfere with the day-to-day administration of sport.

The area in which UNESCO and the IOC can work together, or at least in mutual acknowledgement and harmony, is with the Third World. In the context of the Olympic Movement this means three areas: Central and Caribbean America, Africa, and Asia. The term "Afro-Asian" is a misnomer loosely employed to describe that less-privileged group of people as against the developed world of Europe and North America, the cradles of modern international sport. The first Olympic person to see a need to provide sporting aid and assistance, to develop not only skills but attitudes too, was Count de Beaumont. With private money he had collected, he initiated a fund for this purpose that was eventually taken over by the IOC under the name Olympic Solidarity, which comes from the French but to the English-speaking world has a connotation of left-wing trade unions and the Polish uprising in 1980.

The funds for Solidarity come through the growing television contracts for showing the Games. A considerable percentage goes into the Solidarity fund, which is used by the NOCs in part to organise coaching courses, in conjunction with the federations, in Olympic sports in various countries.

The national Olympic committees were originally formed solely to enter competitors in the Olympic Games. Most have evolved to assist in the development of all sport in between the periods of the Games, besides selecting and training potential Olympic athletes. Some, like the French Olympic committee (CNOSF), combine the duties of an NOC with those of a sports council or a confederation of many sports besides those included in the Olympic Games. The IOC states that on Olympic matters Olympic sports representatives must have the majority vote, but it is expected that NOCs will interest themselves in a far broader range of activities than entries and fund raising for the Olympic Games.

Giulio Onesti, the late president of the Italian NOC (CONI) and the IOC member for Italy, was the first to summon the NOCs together in a general assembly prefixed with the word "permanent," its first president being Mario Vázquez Raña, president of the Mexican NOC. The NOCs had always met regularly with the Executive Board of the IOC. When Brundage addressed the national Olympic committees at their meeting with the Executive Board at Tehran in 1957, I was sitting as president of an NOC in the body of the hall and I shuddered with embarrassment when he referred to us as the IOC's children. The attitude was that of paternalistic patronage, as if we were all incapable of thinking for ourselves. It was this approach that led to the formation of the Assembly of National Olympic Committees and the union of the sports under the banner of ANOC and GAIF (the General Assembly of International Federations). Had his approach been different, the relationship among the IOC, the NOCs and the IFs would have been more compatible, as they are now; although bodies such as ANOC and GAIF are extremely useful, whether on a permanent or an *ad hoc* basis, for the coordination of the common interests of either the international federations or the national Olympic committees. There can be triplication of work if it is not coordinated and the terms of reference clearly drawn.

There are considerable differences among the IFs. Most of them, like the NOCs, are restricted by their finances. A strong president can make or break a federation. There is an ever-increasing desire by individuals for personal self-aggrandisement, and this perhaps does not always attract the best leaders to sport.

Among individual nations, some in West Africa, such as Zaire and Togo, are more inclined to beg for assistance than promote their own ideas. This will change as their sports leaders gain confidence over the years. The colonial powers left little behind them in the way of sporting tradition, and one cannot help comparing the African distance runners, boxers, and soccer players, excellent though some of them are, with their counterparts among the black Americans, who have benefited so much from the facilities and assistance provided by voluntary effort in the United States and who, in consequence, triumph in many major sporting events.

The progress of sport in the Third World depends very much on the president of each NOC, as well as on the members of the IOC in each area and territory. The African members of the IOC are of all colours and races. Although still few in number, they have all contributed actively to the spreading of the Olympic Movement throughout their continent. However, the movement towards independence has made it difficult to find enough Third World candidates and the IOC is very much underrepresented in Africa as a result. I hope that will change.

Ahmed Touny, the IOC member for Egypt, who negotiated with the Palestinians at Munich, was a member of his country's parliament with a great knowledge of sport. Mohammed Mzali, a Tunisian, is a moderate in politics who has always spoken out against boycotts. On two occasions—in Montreal and Moscow—his NOC's team did not compete. He braved considerable opposition and hostility when he attacked the withdrawal of the African teams, including his own, as a means of protest. In Moscow his position must have been even more difficult for, by then, he was his country's premier. Also there were Sir Ade Ademola and Reginald Alexander, already referred to in Chapter V.

Dr. Abdel Mohamed Halim is the IOC member for the Sudan, and Ydnekatchew Tessema represents us in Ethiopia. They are both closely connected with FIFA and soccer. This is the most popular game throughout Africa, because it is cheap, it can be played easily, and it is a game in which many people can take part.

There have been strong arguments for removing all team games from the Olympic programme, because they do not express the individualism associated with the ancient games and, to a certain extent, with the beginning of the modern. Soccer has come under particular attack because of its professional World Cup competition. However, we must nurture the enthusiasm and skill that African and other Third World countries show for Olympic sports. Therefore, as long as there is consideration for such sports as softball and other events that are not strongly represented in Third World countries, soccer, which *is* worldwide, must retain its place on the programme.

Halim has had a distinguished career, not only in medicine,

which he studied in London, but also in the evolution of the Sudan. Tessema's country has changed from the days of Emperor Haile Selassie to its present condition as a socialist state, in which he is minister for youth and sport. Such men must have political sentiments, however much they may try to set them aside. I myself found difficulty in disregarding my own political and, indeed, religious feelings, as is essential in an international organisation like the IOC. To do so successfully takes a strong mind and will.

The Third World has been exploited for political purposes by both East and West. But certainly the East has been far more vigorous and successful in this exploitation than its rival. It has more often accompanied efforts of aggressive economic, social, political, and military aid with sports aid.

At the African Games of Lagos in 1973, West Germany was responsible for building the stadium and East Germany for training the athletes for the show business of the opening and closing events. In 1979 I found in the small West African State of Benin one hundred mainland Chinese supervising and several thousand natives building a vast 60,000-capacity stadium, where perhaps some simpler form of aid might have been more useful. Also, in Asia the previous year I saw the Chinese building a stadium in Pakistan's capital, Islamabad.

Though the French, as Coubertin pointed out, were always behind in their pedagogical outlook on sport, it is in former French colonies that sport appears most progressive. The exceptions are former British possessions, Nigeria and Kenya, where the new leaders have taken an active part in the development of sporting facilities.

It is impossible for every sport to be practised in every country. Therefore the developing countries should limit their ambitions to those sports in which natural ability enables them to show most prowess and which are most appropriate to their social and economic conditions.

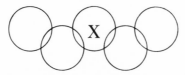

Women and the Olympic Movement

At the 1982 session of the IOC in Rome, Pirjo Haggman of Finland and Flor Isave Fonseca of Venezuela took the oath to become the first women members of the IOC.

When I became president in Munich I did not unfold any grandiose plans for change, but I did say I could see no reason why women should not take their place in the IOC. Although I was not going to pick a few token ladies just to make my point, I did have several potential members in mind.

Some of these candidates were, unfortunately, in countries where there were already members. In one instance, the current member withdrew his offer of retirement when he heard he was to be followed by a woman. In other countries there were several suitable male candidates, and I believe in electing the best, regardless of sex.

Such considerations prevented the election of female IOC members until my successor's presidency, particularly as there were no elections of any members at the Moscow session, by agreement of the IOC, in view of other problems and items of business.

While male chauvinism in sport has ruled for a longer period than in the International Olympic Committee, the post of director is held by a woman, Monique Berlioux, who is regarded highly as a formidable person far beyond the sporting spheres of the world. Her Olympic days began in 1948 when she swam for France in the Games in London. Twenty years later she was appointed to take charge of press relations for the IOC. I was a member of the interviewing panel. She was wheeled in on a chair, but her incapacity was merely temporary—I think it was a broken leg. The following year, 1968, Johan Westerhoff, the first full-time secretary of the IOC, resigned. No replacement was appointed and his work fell upon the shoulders of Berlioux, whose qualities quickly began to emerge.

Monique Berlioux is authoritarian and rules her staff firmly, which is not always appreciated and probably had something to do with the original high turnover of personnel at the Château de Vidy. Yet she maintains a high standard of efficiency. She is staunchly loyal to the IOC and its presidents. She never has any hesitation in expressing her views, especially if she believes a mistake is being made, but once she has done so she carries out instructions with accuracy and speed. She must have been extremely frustrated at some of the muddles that the members created during the sessions.

When I became president I had reservations about Berlioux's suiting my style. I had serious reservations about the organisation of the headquarters and I discussed my views with many members. I wanted initially a director general and, beneath, a press and information director and a technical director. I did not expect she would accept this new structure, having been given so much power by Brundage. However, I am not a man of instant decision and, while giving due time for consideration of these changes, I came to appreciate more the qualities of Berlioux. I have never had cause to regret that I discarded my ideas about a new structure to ensure retaining the dedication and qualities that she brought to her work and her supreme loyalty to me and the IOC during my term of office.

In addition to controlling her staff, the director has responsibility for the arrangement, in association with the host committee, of the sessions of the IOC. This is not always easy; in addition to the joint sessions with the IFs and/or NOCs, there are the annual (in the year of the Games, biannual) sessions of the full IOC. She has also been responsible, together with the IOC's financial and legal advisers, for the negotiation of most of the television contracts, as well as other financial contracts into which the IOC must enter. Whenever I heard complaints about her, they merely satisfied me that she was doing her work; if I had not heard complaints I would have worried that she was yielding to outside pressures, something she would never do. However, she has quite enough subtlety to find compromise solutions to difficult problems when necessary.

In view of the fact women were usually only associated with the administration of women's sport, in no case, to my knowledge, has a woman ever been elected a president of an NOC, although there have been former distinguished Olympic athletes or medical specialists. The same applies to the international federations, with the exception of archery, where the president for the Games of 1972 and 1976 was Mrs. Ingrid Frith, of Danish birth, married and resident in England. She was quiet, determined, and an excellent leader. At all our meetings she made the most constructive statement and suggestions. Her standards were always high (as indeed were the standards of the variety of hats she always wore). She was one of the great Olympic characters.

The Olympic wives are frequently forgotten (and this may apply in the future to the Olympic husbands). They play an important part, especially at the time of the sessions and Games which they attend. I was very unpopular when I restricted the attendance of Olympic widows to ease the situation of the Olympic organising committees of the sessions. Among them were considerable characters who had much influence both on their husbands and, indirectly, on the Olympic Movement; on the other hand there were others who were probably the source of most gossip.

The hostess service for the sessions and Games organised by Dr. Emmy Schwabe of Austria, who was awarded the Bronze Medal of the Olympic Order in 1979, was invaluable. The hostesses were selected from an exclusive social stratum even higher than the older members of the IOC. Without them the members of the IOC would have been lost, both literally and metaphorically, for they acted not only as guides and couriers, but also as interpreters. They saved my wife and myself an immense amount of time and we were always wonderfully looked after and formed friendships still remembered by an array of Christmas cards which arrive each year even from the Soviet Union. One hostess, a German princess, married Avery Brundage as his second wife, while King Carl Gustaf of Sweden married a hostess whom we all knew from the Munich Games.

Bearing in mind the slow emancipation of women in the Western world (in Switzerland it was only recently that all cantons gave the franchise to women), the IOC pioneered in women's participation, and in 1900 (Paris) women competed in golf and tennis, and in 1904 (St. Louis) in archery. Golf is no longer on the programme but tennis competitions are to be reintroduced in 1988, and perhaps names such as Susanne Lenglen of Britain and Helen Wills of the United States will again reverberate as they did in 1920 (Antwerp) and 1924 (Paris). Archery was reintroduced on the programme in 1972 (Munich). In 1912 (Stockholm) women competed in swimming, with the 100-metre freestyle won by F. Durack of Australia and high-board diving by G. Johansson of Sweden. Track and field had to wait until 1928 (Amsterdam), when E. Robinson (United States) won the 100 metres, L. Radke-Batschauer (Germany) the 800 metres, E. Catherwood of Canada the high jump, and H. Konopacka (Poland) the discus. Canada also won the gold medal in the women's 400-metre relay.

As women competed, so have their times improved, from Robinson's 12.2 seconds in the 100 metres in 1928 to the 11.06 of Liyudmila Kondratieva (Soviet Union) in 1980 (Moscow); also the same distance in freestyle swimming has improved from Durack's 1 minute 22.2 seconds in 1912 to Barbara Krause's (East Germany) 54.79 seconds at Moscow. Had the United States been in the competition in many sports in Moscow, it may well have been that many Olympic women's records might have been beaten. This is something that will never be known, although world records are not necessarily achieved at the Olympic Games but also in other competitions.

Today, due to television, women gymnasts—usually very young girls—have attracted the world's attention and such names as Nadia Comaneci (Rumania) and Olga Korbut (Soviet Union) are household names. Rhythmic gymnastics, which are restricted to women, will be included on the Los Angeles programme. Women have participated in canoeing since 1948 and rowing since 1980. In some sports, such as equestrianism and yachting, there is sex equality. Other sports do not include women's events, e.g., boxing, weight lifting, wrestling, and the modern pentathlon, but it is surprising women's events were not scheduled in cycling until 1984, or in judo until 1988. Shooting was a joint nondiscriminatory sport, but classes are now being introduced for women. If men and women can compete equally in a sport it is preferable, but the recommendation for women's participation rests first of all with the federation's progress. The marathon, with the necessity of clearing the streets, is always a problem. It was intended in Los Angeles to have men and women competing at the same time in this event, but now two separate races are to be run.

During my term of office, women's hockey (grass) was introduced. Here I thought was a problem as the IOC only recognises one international federation in a sport and it was necessary to bring together the International Hockey Federation with its equivalent controlling women to form a joint body for Olympic purposes. The women's hockey organisers are, sadly, the reverse of male chauvinists and wish to retain their independence.

There is no doubt there has been discrimination or possibly conservative thinking in sports in which women can participate, and if they do not participate their potential number of individual administrators is less. Prior to Rome in 1960, I was criticised by the then-conservative Catholic archbishop of Dublin, Dr. John Charles McQuaid, for endorsing the entry of Ireland's first woman Olympic athlete (Maeve Kyle) into the arena to compete in the 100-metre and 200-metre running events. He was shocked at a housewife running in public in shorts. (Incidentally, she was not of his denomination.) There are certain ethnic and religious groups, such as the Muslims, who have a certain philosophy regarding the place of women. Changes are welcome but I do not think there has been so much chauvinistic discrimination as a lack of imagination, forethought, and respect for women.

In the Winter Games, women have participated since the Second World War in downhill skiing and the slalom, besides Nordic skiing; in the Winter Games, figure skating and ice dancing are the equivalent of gymnastics in the summer. At least the modern International Olympic Committee as founded by Coubertin has not followed the Hellenic tradition of not allowing women even to view the ancient Games.

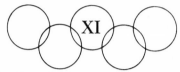

Professionalism Versus Amateurism

Pierre de Coubertin was not opposed to the idea that the few most elite Olympic competitors should receive some recompense. But his principal aim, which was well in advance of his time, was to encourage "sport for all." The British Empire, then at its zenith, attributed much virtue to the combination of sport and scholarship—the stock-in-trade of their public schools. If you did not shine at games you could receive a good education, but you were not likely to reach the pinnacle of responsibility and fame. This tradition greatly influenced Coubertin.

Since 1896 the question of amateurism and professionalism has continued to be debated. Professionalism is easy to define: it means that a sportsman or athlete is paid for his performance or for teaching, and that this payment constitutes his principal means of livelihood. Nonprofessionalism is different. The word "amateur" has become devalued because of the difficulty in defining just what it means. To describe someone as an amateur because he does something for love rather than commercial gain is no longer exact. The word has frequently come to mean somebody who does something rather badly.

The ICC has been discussing the question of amateurism since its inception. Avery Brundage believed fanatically that a true Olympic champion must be "pure" to such a degree that he or she could not even receive payment for "broken time" (loss of earnings) or more than essential expenses for travel and accommodation for competitions.

The Eastern Europeans, in particular, continue as strong upholders of the policy of pure amateurism since they have no commercial sponsorship of competitors—a function performed by the state—and few recognised professionals. Yet most Westerners consider all Eastern European athletes as professionals because, during their period of peak performance, they are exempted from other employment. Eastern Europeans consider only those Westerners who receive payment professionals.

The twilight zone between a high-performance athlete released by a company for international competition for an unlimited time—for instance, Herb Elliot, the Australian runner, who worked for Shell and subsequently went to Cambridge—and an athlete sponsored by a commercial firm is very difficult to define. Personally I can see no difference between the two; nor can I see much difference between the competitor sponsored by the state and one sponsored by private sources. It is important that all contracts and agreements should be in accordance with the IF rules, as well as with those of the IOC, and should be administered by the IFs or NOCs as far as the Olympic competitors are concerned.

There are untold stories and myths about "appearance money." Some athletes have been honest enough to admit that they have received money; in some cases they have been disenfranchised as a result. At least we have progressed from the days in 1948 when a Swedish dressage team was disqualified. In those days commissioned officers were considered amateurs and other military ranks professionals, so a Swedish warrant officer on the team was given a temporary commission, from which he reverted after competing. The medals were withdrawn from the Swedish team.

The case of Jim Thorpe, who had taken negligible amounts of money in the period before the Games for playing in a minor American baseball competition, has been a running sore ever since his disqualification as an Olympic champion after the 1912 Games. Although he died in 1953, there are still powerful pressure groups demanding his reinstatement. It is an emotional case, as Thorpe's relations continue to feel very strongly about it. Moreover Thorpe was an Indian, which is an aggravating factor because it introduces other social and political issues.

The matter was usually raised at election time, when political popularity is of paramount importance in the United States. Thorpe certainly did not make a fortune out of sport and was, in his time, the greatest athlete in the world. Yet, however sympathetic one was, there is no rule permitting his reinstatement, and the American Olympic officials have been firmly against setting a precedent some seventy years after the event, as has been the IAAF.

Since my ceasing my presidency, my successor agreed to create this precedent. This pleased me as far as Jim Thorpe was concerned, but I feel it may give rise to further appeals in future. (It was in a congressional election year, 1982.)

Though the definition of amateurism had thus plagued the Olympic Movement throughout its history, it was not until the 1970's that the issue was brought to a head and the rules revised.

In 1971 the IOC had three European vice-presidents: Count de Beaumont, Herman van Karnebeek, and myself. We were appointed by Brundage to discuss various matters with the IFs, with whom Brundage and the IOC had little contact. We met the presidents and secretaries-general of the federations in Lausanne, Paris, and London. One of the objects of our enquiry was the question of amateurism, which was defined very differently from federation to federation. Where equipment was involved, such as horses, yachts, or skis, exploitation for commercial purposes was manifest. In the case of skiing there was the added interest of the tourist trade. It was the first time we had met the federation heads individually and they had been given the opportunity to put their problems to us individually rather than as a group. It was quite incredible that in the seventies we should be doing this for the first time and finally coming closer to the roots of the amateurism problem, which was not about one rule or attitude but rather about the way each sport had evolved and wanted to go on evolving in spite of the strict Olympic code. We came to understand the complexities of these problems and all agreed there should be changes.

As we travelled we held press conferences that showed the direction of our thinking about the then rigid amateur codes, which were being broken by a very large number of competitors, not only in the Olympic Games but in many other competitions. Finally, in Lausanne, we discussed with the IFs how to retain the principles of amateurism but, at the same time, move with the changing times.

Brundage then appeared on one of his infrequent and unexpected visits there. I think it was the press reports of our activities that brought him to Lausanne in such haste. He was obviously angry and concerned that we might be undermining his authority. He realised that he had been bypassed and that he should really have done this himself if he wanted to maintain his original position. But it was too late for that, because too much was now out in the open. The federations had found a new rapport and their meetings led to radical changes.

After much consideration and discussion with the IFs, the eligibility rule was altered to read as follows:

Eligibility Code
To be eligible to participate in the Olympic Games a competitor must:
—Observe and abide by the rules of the IOC and, in addition, the rules of his or her International Federation as approved by the IOC, even if the Federation's rules are more strict than those of the IOC.
—Not receive any financial rewards and material benefits in connection with his or her sports participation except as permitted in the bye-laws to this rule.

The bye-laws, without saying so, accept broken time in the Olympic Games. They permit a competitor to be a physical education or sports teacher giving elementary instruction and, during the period of preparation for actual competition, to accept prizes won in competition within the rules established by each federation, and to accept academic and technical scholarships, which were anathema to my predecessor.

Some IFs wanted the bye-laws suppressed totally and only the rule retained, with the IOC approving or disapproving the rules of any sport that we wished to include on the Olympic programme. This is the way I think things will evolve. But, at the time, no sooner had this been suggested by certain federations than others came to me and said they must have guidelines. The IAAF had always been guided by the rules of the

IOC, as it held no world championships other than at the time of the Olympic Games. This is changing; a world competition has been instituted with the athletes competing by invitation and now there are also separate world championships. Thus the IAAF no longer has the strict Olympic rules on which to fall back if it so wishes.

There is one point on which I admit defeat. It was always my belief that a competitor could be a professional at one sport and a nonprofessional in another. An example in non-Olympic sports is a professional racing motorist who plays golf as an amateur. Should he be ineligible to play in amateur golf tournaments? It is quite possible, and has happened, that a professional rider employed in a stable for training horses finds himself in his spare time in the local amateur boxing club. It seems strange that he should be excluded from Olympic or international nonprofessional boxing because he spends his day riding and training horses for pay. When this situation arises a blind eye is turned to it. Yet this has damaged the credibility of nonprofessional sport and the Olympic Games. The sooner this is changed the better.

When motor cars first came on the roads they were preceded by a man with a red flag. Today there is no flag, but there are rules regarding the speed at which cars can travel for reasons of safety and, more recently, to conserve fuel. It is equally important for sportsmen to maintain the principles but vary the details according to changing circumstances. Men and women are living longer; there has been a complete social and economic transformation, in both capitalist and Communist countries; there is an ever-increasing interest in sport that must be taken into account. When we were able to change the rules between 1972 and Montreal, a considerable step forward was taken, but it was not enough.

There was a question of further changing the eligibility rule prior to Moscow, but it was the feeling of the IOC that the current regulations should stand for some time to see how things would work out. From the Olympic Games' point of view they worked reasonably well. For some federations this did not make an iota of difference, because their rules were stricter, while others, such as the IAAF, found severe problems. The equestrian federation resolved the issue by declaring many of their competitors, especially in Britain, professionals. Possibly some of these were declared professionals before the new eligibility rule was established and could have remained eligible for the Olympic Games under the more liberal framework. Most federations do not permit a reinstated amateur to compete, as is the case under the Olympic rules.

Since the IOC session following the congress in 1981, the eligibility rule has again been changed to read more simply and to give greater latitude between the IOC and the federations. Also it has been made more definite than the unclear rule I inherited in 1972.

When elected president, I was asked by the press whether the Olympic Games would ever be "open," i.e., for professionals and amateurs. Unfortunately, I replied harshly, "Never"; from then onwards I have never used the word "never." There must be a continual evolution with attention to the different social conditions for each sport. Competition is the right of all rather than that of the privileged alone, as at the end of the last century. As I write, the IOC continues to make realistic progress under my successor.

Another area of conflict closely associated with eligibility is in advertising. Currently an Olympic competitor may be used in an advertisement provided the contract is with the national federation or NOC. My own belief is that all these contracts should be strictly controlled by the national federations or NOCs with the approval of the IOC or IFs. This would lessen the danger of athletes' falling into the hands of entrepreneurial agents who will let them appear only when the manager thinks he is going to get the largest financial return. But, knowing the way the business world works, I admit it will be difficult to combat the commercial intrusion. This happened in tennis at Wimbledon—a pro-am event with great prestige that has retained its high competition level. In the past, after Wimbledon, many of the top players would come to Dublin to play in the All-Ireland Championships and then go on to other smaller events in Europe. Many of these have disappeared and been replaced by commercial events. The best professionals return directly to the United States, where the prize money is far larger, and so the best players are no longer seen in Dublin. Tennis is now returning to the official programme, in 1988, and will certainly create eligibility problems.

Sponsorship of competitions is another practice that came and this leads to conflicts, particularly in Europe, between East and West. A sponsor wishes to obtain the maximum publicity in return for his large financial outlay, and so stadiums are festooned with the signs of permanent contractual obligations, while the sponsor seeks to have his name in an agreed size on the competitor's clothing. This is in order for most federations providing it does not conflict with the television contract.

I recall going to the European track and field competitions in Rome in 1974, which were being televised by Italian television and taken by most European nations. A large amount of additional space had been sold in the arena. The Germans refused to transmit this competition because of the promotional aspect. This was unfair to the German viewers and the sport concerned, but was, from a commercial point of view, understandable. At this event the advertising included slogans for the British Labour party in the period just before an election. These were subsequently removed as there should be no political demonstrations at events controlled by the IAAF. Buying space for a political party constitutes a political demonstration.

Moreover, tobacco and drink firms are not acceptable now as new sponsors, although they may retain sponsorship of events with which they are already connected. As a director of a brewery and chairman of a tobacco company, I am sensitive to the important responsibility that devolves on these companies. Further, there are athletes who, in principle, do not wish to carry sponsorship tabs, while the increasing number of Muslim competitors makes the objection to alcohol not only a question of health but also one of religious belief.

These problems will loom very large in Los Angeles, where the Games will be run on a self-financing commercial basis. The United States leads the world in advertising. Madison Avenue is its heart and Los Angeles, with its film-making past, is the principal centre for the show business interests of all the commercial television companies.

The IOC, which has gained great prestige in the world, has

suffered through the ambitions of certain sports and sportsmen, many of whom may well eventually become Olympic competitors. Proof of accusations of sponsorship or appearance money at non-Olympic competitions is always difficult to obtain. I have been given names, read articles, made enquiries, but evidence cannot be obtained without a private police force, which is out of the question. If the Olympic Movement cannot be administered honestly, then the future is bleak. It will not be changed overnight, but it must be improved from sport to sport by the IOC's intervention with the IFs and NOCs, if the ideal for which we are all striving is to be upheld.

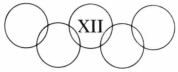

On Slippery Slopes to Los Angeles

The American-Olympic con-
nection in my time has not been a very happy one. A few
months after my election as president, Denver withdrew from
the position of city for the Olympic Winter Games of 1976. In
Montreal the U.S. Olympic Committee (USOC) threatened to
withdraw (taking the television contract with them) if Taiwan
was not allowed to compete. Staging the 1980 Winter Games in
a tiny place like Lake Placid, N.Y., was a mistake that brought
the Olympic Movement unhappy publicity, and Los Angeles
has the Games of 1984 on an agreement that the IOC may still
come to rue.

When Denver reported in 1972 to the IOC at the time of
the Munich Games, there were already indications that we
might run into problems because of an environmental preserva-
tion order. Also the official report indicated that one of the
mountains designated for alpine skiing was inauspiciously
called Evergreen, which does not give an impression of snow.
Finally, Denver would not have a bobsled run, though they had
been awarded the Games on evidence that they had all the necessary facilities. Instead, the bob events would now have to take
place some hundreds of miles away in Lake Placid. This was
going to cause a disruption that had not been envisaged when
the IOC members voted for Denver at Amsterdam in 1970.
What was really alarming was that opposition to the Games on
ecological as well as financial grounds had arisen in the city of
Denver itself, and we now heard for the first time that a referen-

dum was to be held to decide whether Denver should play host to the Games. Since it had already contracted to do so, this announcement came as a bombshell.

I shall always remember the confidence and panache with which the Denver delegation made the original bid for the Games. Now the organising committee tried to play down the referendum. "This has not been unusual in the United States and the Committee was confident the Bill would be unsuccessful. If this happened the opposition would die down and everyone would welcome the athletes to Denver," they reported to the IOC.

Marc Hodler, a member of the IOC for Switzerland and president of the International Ski Federation (FIS), argued realistically that the IOC would be most unwise to continue on the assumption that Denver would be the site of the Games, and maintained that there were other cities that would be prepared to take them over.

He was right. In spite of the optimism of the Denver delegation, clearly the city was about to pull out, and when the referendum took place on November 8, 1972, this is what happened. The voting went against the organising committee, which had to withdraw from the undertaking. In an article published in a magazine called *Colorado* in January 1973, a local voter was quoted as saying: "I didn't vote against the Olympic Games, I voted against the politicians and arrogant organisers; against their smugness, secrecy and bungling and against the promoters and hucksters who were jumping in for a fast buck. It is too bad. I think the Olympics themselves could have been really great. I don't expect we will see another chance like this in a lifetime."

No sooner were the results of the referendum known than a court case was brought by a group of people against the Denver organising committee. Its outcome clinched the matter and the following cable, addressed to me by the mayor, formally conveyed the organising committee's decision: AM NOW PERMITTED TO CONVEY THE FACT THAT VOTERS APPROVED AMENDMENT TO CONSTITUTION OF STATE OF COLORADO AND CHARTER OF CITY AND COUNTY OF DENVER PROHIBITING EXPENDITURE OF STATE AND CITY FUNDS FOR 1976 WINTER OLYMPIC GAMES. AS A RESULT

THE [ORGANISING COMMITTEE] HAS DETERMINED IT HAS NO CHOICE BUT TO WITHDRAW INVITATION TO HOLD GAMES IN DENVER.

The IOC had an agreement with Denver but no legal contract—the last time that situation was to exist. Since then, each city that stages the Games signs a legal contract with the IOC so that the Olympic Movement is properly protected from people who embark on such a venture without exploring all the ramifications. The USOC must, of course, bear some of the blame in this matter since it approved Denver's application in the first place.

In any event, the voters of Colorado, known as "Ski Country, U.S.A.," had summarily rejected the most prestigious winter sports events in the world. They sent the 1976 Winter Games packing. Nothing like this had ever happened before. In light of it, Brundage would have used all his power to disband the Winter Games, but I knew, after consulting reliable members of my Executive Board, that the overwhelming majority wished them to go on.

On November 15, 1972, we began searching for another city for the 1976 Winter Olympic Games, which were just over three years away. All NOCs and IFs were alerted about the situation. I decided that the board would choose another candidate in February 1973, in Lausanne, where we would have all the winter sports federations and the representatives of the candidate cities together.

A number of sites were considered. Mont Blanc in France had a disadvantage in that the Games would have had to be held over a scattered area. Tampere was worse placed still; there are no mountains in Finland and therefore the alpine skiing events would have had to take place in another country, a situation not covered by IOC rules. Lake Placid and Innsbruck had hosted the Games before, Lake Placid in 1932 and Innsbruck in 1964.

The Lake Placid delegation making the bid before the board included assorted sporting and governmental officials and a remarkable gentleman called the Reverend Bernard Fell. Described as chairman of the organising committee, though presumably his correct title should have been chairman-designate, he had come to preaching as a late vocation, and whether or not he was making up for lost time, he was certainly the most persuasive speaker I have ever heard. He explained that all the facilities already existed at Lake Placid and would need only a little modification, and that having been the site of many national and international winter sports events, his town would obviously be the perfect choice for the Winter Olympic Games.

The extremely impressive performance of its delegation at this meeting made Lake Placid the favourite and ultimately the victor three years later, when the Winter Games of 1980 were being allotted. At Lausanne in February 1973, however, the members of the Executive Board prudently decided to entrust the Games of 1976 to Innsbruck, which everybody felt sure would be well able to organise them, being the capital of the Tirol and having all the facilities to hand. The decision was a wise one.

I was frightened that Lake Placid was going to be successful with a very plausible bid but there were members of the board, sufficient as it turned out, who felt that the movement had behaved tactlessly over the Schranz affair in 1972 at the Winter Games in Sapporo, and wanted an opportunity to make peace with the people of Austria.

At Sapporo, Karl Schranz, a skiing hero in Austria, was disqualified, largely at the instigation of Brundage, after Schranz was alleged to have admitted in an interview in the Olympic Village that he had received money for competing. Schranz was sent home before the Games were finished and when he arrived back in Vienna it was estimated that there were a million people to greet him. However, the decision to give the Games to Innsbruck did not need this emotional content; it was the correct one in the circumstances and the city discharged its responsibilities in the proper manner.

The USOC, having mishandled one application for the Winter Olympic Games, almost did the same thing four years later when it was first announced that Salt Lake City was to be the candidate for the Games of 1980. That seemed to be a domestic misunderstanding and, after some sorting out, Lake Placid presented itself to the IOC as the candidate at Vienna in 1974. This was the session at which Los Angeles and Moscow were making application for the Summer Games. A very strong bid was made, the chief speaker again being Fell, the persuasive preacher.

At the time Lake Placid seemed an appropriate choice. As far as the facilities for the competitors were concerned (particularly the technical requirements), it matched up to most needs. But Lake Placid was inevitably to lose the battle of coping with a large number of people in a small space. The transport system never worked properly and, while there were mitigating circumstances for this—labour problems necessitating the import of buses from Canada—the logistics of moving the required number of people to a variety of sites was never going to work.

Los Angeles had continually sought to repeat the successful Games of 1932, and the *ad hoc* local Olympic committee under an enthusiastic spokesman, lawyer John Argue, had worked undaunted by a previous lack of success. When the Los Angeles bid for the Games of 1984 was made it was very different to the previous two. In 1970 the Californians appeared short on experience. At Vienna four years later, they appeared resigned to a Soviet victory, although disappointed. But in preparation for the allocation of the 1984 Games, which was to be made in Athens at the session of 1978, they prepared a document that was uncompromising in its demands, perhaps because they thought as the only candidate they could dictate. In effect, they said that the Games would be run their way and there was to be little account taken of the rules of the IOC or its traditions and protocol.

Ordinarily we would have issued a polite rejection and turned aside the show business people behind the application. However, the Olympic Movement in 1978 was at a low ebb, with the aftermath of Montreal still being felt sharply. Some people believed that the Olympic Games were becoming too large and that they were grinding to a halt, but the fact that the Moscow celebration was but two years away and that all was proceeding smoothly made me, and many of my members, feel that we should try to bring the Los Angeles group round to a point where they were closer to the Olympic spirit and thus eligible for staging the Games. The one aspect which worried many members, but not myself, was the premise of the bid, which was that the city of Los Angeles would not be responsible for the Games, making no financial contribution whatsoever. The organising committee, a consortium of businessmen, would run the Games at a profit, which would be used for the development of sport in the United States.

After the costs that the city of Montreal had incurred and stories about a billion-dollar deficit and legal enquiries into corruption, it did not seem credible that the IOC should contemplate such an offer. But there was, of course, a vast difference between Montreal and Los Angeles. To begin with, Los Angeles had many more facilities. It also had two universities, which could be used as two Villages, although only one was then contemplated.

In many respects the organising committee members intended to run the Games in much the way previous organising committees had done, although they were frank about the differences from the beginning. Previously, commercialism and the type of contracts into which the organising committee entered might have been construed to be against the Olympic principles, if not actually against the rules. In the case of Los Angeles they were explicit that they were going to run the Games as a commercial company.

I felt that once the original arrogance of "We'll run our Games our way" had been removed, the Los Angeles group shared our vision for the future of the Olympic Movement. Their original application was rejected at the Athens session, but the 1984 Games were provisionally awarded to them, subject to their entering into a contract according to Olympic rules. Over the next ten months it was agreed that there should be two contracts, one between the IOC and the organising committee, which would take on the responsibility normally vested in a city, and one between the organising committee and the USOC. It took much negotiating to achieve a position in which each party found the outcome satisfactory. The biggest stumbling block in terms of delay was brought about by the need for the USOC, rightly, to be indemnified against the possible financial failure of the organising committee.

When in January 1979 agreement still had not been

reached, the IOC began looking for new bids. The USOC, however, wanted to be safe rather than sorry, for it and not the IOC was going to be the responsible party. Finally, there were two "signings." Mayor Tom Bradley of Los Angeles, for whom I had great respect, could not under any circumstances become financially involved, but wanted to show the world that Los Angeles and the United States supported the Games. So we agreed that we would go to Washington, D.C., to meet President Carter and exchange unsigned letters of agreement. (Carter actually got no closer than the next room in the White House, where he was dealing with Arab-Israeli problems.) The final contracts were not signed until March 1979, and by then there was considerable pressure from some members to call for new bids. A year had been lost but if there was catching up to do it seems that Los Angeles has already done so.

My one doubt about Los Angeles, which remains, concerns transportation. The city is an enormous sprawl and the sites are widely spread. While the freeways and highways provide excellent connections, they are overloaded at peak periods. My prayer is that no 1984 Olympian will hand down a story to his grandchildren about the traffic jam that kept him out of the competition. The subsequent decision to have two main Olympic Villages has brought criticism from some NOCs, particularly the Soviets, who must have forgotten their demand for a separate village at Helsinki, which was granted. Staging the rowing and canoeing on a natural lake has saved the expense of building an artificial one as promised in the bid, but means that these competitors will also be housed sixty miles away from the Olympic family.

The organising committee has promised Spartan Games and, at the time of writing, there has been no unnecessary junketing or promotion. It is important that the needs of the IFs and NOCs are met, but without waste on luxury.

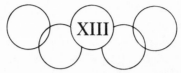

The Chinese and Other Political Puzzles

From the moment I was elected president I wanted the whole of China to compete in the Olympic arena. It was, I felt, a curious anomaly that the country with the world's largest population did not take part in the Games. And I worked for years to change this.

The Chinese problem had long dogged the Olympic Movement. Chinese politicians were anxious to use the Olympic Movement for their own tactical ends, and the matter was further complicated by the names their governments used. The People's Republic of China has its capital in Peking. The Republic of China, commonly referred to as Nationalist China, is based in Taipei on the island of Taiwan.

Before the Second World War the Chinese Olympic Committee had its headquarters in Nanking. But in 1949, when Mao Tse-tung came into power in Peking, the Chiang Kai-shek government left the mainland and set up its capital in Taipei. The committee then split, the majority of members moving with Chiang Kai-shek to Taipei. They claimed to be the original Olympic committee recognised by the IOC and, until much later, claimed also to control sport, *de jure,* through all China, including the mainland. (There was, of course, no chance of their controlling it *de facto.*) At the same time another Chinese NOC, also claiming to be the true one, established itself in Peking.

At the time of my election in 1952 to the IOC, it contained no fewer than three Chinese members—Dr. C. T. Wang, elected in 1922, Dr. H. H. Kung, elected in 1939, and Shou Yi-tung, elected in 1947. Wang and Kung were both supporters of Chiang Kai-shek, Kung being married to a sister of Mme. Chiang. Shou, who had considerable experience in sports education and administration, supported the Mao government. Thus not only was the Chinese NOC split between Peking and Taipei, but the Chinese members of the IOC were also at loggerheads. Yet the address of the Chinese Olympic Committee remained officially in Nanking. No trace can be found of any notification of its move to Taipei.

Compounding this confusion was the fact that the IOC had not stuck to its own rules by which only NOCs recognised by the IOC could make entries. In 1952, although the officially recognised Chinese Olympic Committee was now in Taipei, thirty-eight men and two women went from Peking to take part in the Helsinki Games. Since there was no recognised Olympic committee in Peking their entries, strictly speaking, must have been out of order. Yet they were allowed to compete. Subsequently, an Olympic committee with headquarters in Peking was recognised by the IOC under the name of the Olympic Committee of the Republic of China, as opposed to that which had moved to Taipei. The IOC therefore recognised two Olympic committees in one country or territory, both of which claimed to represent the whole of China.

The Peking committee refused to recognise "two Chinas," in keeping with the policy of the government, which claimed control over all China, including Taiwan; thus there were no mainland Chinese competitors at Melbourne in 1956 and the long break had begun.

Shou Yi-tung, the Maoist member, at the 1957 session of the IOC in Sofia, requested that the committee he represented be known as that of the People's Democratic Republic of China, which was agreed and accepted. Unfortunately he added some provocative political statements about the IOC's recognition of the committee in Taipei, and was called to order by Brundage. Because of the continued recognition of the Chinese Olympic Committee in Taipei, the Olympic Committee of the People's Democratic Republic of China withdrew from the Olympic Movement the following year and Shou resigned from the IOC. All contact, therefore, was now lost with mainland China. No mainland Chinese member of the IOC attended its sessions and none appeared to be active in China. In addition to this, the split within the Chinese NOC was reflected in the international federations, some of which recognised the committee in Taipei and others that in Peking.

At the session of the IOC in Munich in May 1959, the Chinese problem was reviewed. I intervened for the first time on the Chinese question, which had interested me since my days as a young reporter during the Sino-Japanese conflict in 1937. To continue to call the committee in Taipei the Chinese Olympic Committee seemed to me unreasonable and I proposed that, as the name inferred that the administration of sport was for all China, it should be changed. Therefore, in an effort to enable all athletes to compete, we told the Taipei committee to enter the 1960 Games in Rome under the name Formosa. But, as they passed the presidential box in Rome, the athletes from Taiwan unfurled a banner with the words UNDER PROTEST. Again the IOC did not obey its own rules forbidding political demonstrations in the arena, and a chance was missed to sanction this Olympic committee and bring the matter back for general consideration.

Meanwhile, I was offering support for private overtures by individuals on the IOC to influential parties in Peking. This was necessarily going on behind Brundage's back, because some of us felt that the president's views were those of the U.S. State Department, which at the time did not recognise mainland China. In fact his pro-Taiwan attitude was even stronger than America's. For almost ten years the slow, largely secretive talks with people in Peking went on. Then Brundage got wind of them and in one action—the appointment of Henry Hsu to membership in the IOC, utterly against our rules and spirit— put the clock back almost ten years. A Canton-born sportsman, Hsu had been present with his elegant wife as a guest at some of the IOC sessions, although naturally they were not allowed into any meetings or the social functions. Hsu made very close contact with Brundage and if some of us had been a little sharper we would have been aware of what the president was up to, although, on reflection, I do not think we could have divined the details.

At the IOC session in Amsterdam in 1970, when I was on

the Executive Board, Brundage, who throughout supported Taipei against Peking on the grounds that only Peking was acting for political motives, proposed Hsu, who had an address in Taipei, for membership in the IOC. The unwritten protocol of selecting new members is that it is the president who makes discreet enquiries in that part of the world where the new member is required. The president always discusses a potential candidate with other members, particularly those of the Executive Board, and a retiring member's suggestion carries special weight in choosing his successor. Ultimately the name or names are presented to the Executive Board and these are, in general, accepted and ratified at a full session by all the members.

Hsu's nomination was opposed unanimously by the board, the only instance of this happening in my experience. Most of us knew of the quiet overtures with "the other side" and realised that Brundage's move would bring the work of the past ten years crashing down. It was an extremely prolonged and delicate matter and, as some members of the board argued, acceptance of Hsu would immediately be seen as support for one side against the other. The board members decided not to recommend him.

At the full session, when the item on the agenda "New members" was taken, Brundage read out the list and added that of Hsu. Lord Exeter, sitting on his left, shouted, "We did not recommend Mr. Hsu!" and others indicated their support, but Brundage ignored us and Hsu became a member. In a club of gentlemen, rebellion against such autocracy did not occur and, had it done so, would have been ineffectual in this instance.

Beforehand Brundage, determined to have his way, had asked the late George Vargas of the Philippines to canvass those members who might be in favour of Hsu. I later saw the list of supporters and realised that of the members present at the session it amounted to the majority Brundage wanted. So the slim backdoor lines linking the IOC with Peking were snapped. It took years of patient, delicate negotiation before the absurd anomaly of the world's largest population group being left outside the movement was ended. I took the opportunity to start repairing the damage when I attended the Asian Games at Tehran in 1974. By then the Asian Games Federation recognised Peking and not Taipei, so the mainland competitors took part in events at Tehran. I also ensured that they attended an Olympic seminar that was held at the time of the Asian Games and that I opened. I knew that they would regard this as a positive gesture of acceptance. It was at that moment I resolved to do my best to solve the Chinese puzzle and get the mainland back into the Olympic arena. This was to cause immense trouble to my colleagues and myself at the Montreal Games in 1976. (The resulting tangle of political pressures and threats is explained in Chapter XIV on Montreal.)

In 1977 I decided to appoint a commission to examine the Chinese problem and visit both areas in order to write a report. In picking my team I thought I had selected a well-balanced trio in Lance Cross of New Zealand, Tony Bridge from Jamaica, and Alexandru Siperco, our member in Rumania. But I made a mistake. Their conflicting views on the rights and wrongs of the two sides made it impossible for them to offer objective suggestions. Siperco, in fact, could not travel to Taipei because his government wouldn't let him, which I suppose I would have known if I had done my homework better.

I therefore undertook the work of the commission myself. I went to Peking in September 1977 with Masaji Kiyokawa, the IOC member for Japan, and the technical director of the IOC, the late Harry Banks, where we met the All-China Sports Federation officers. There was a lot of worthwhile talking but I think many of my members felt that I should have immediately gone to Taipei. I delayed this part of my plan for a year and went, eventually with Louis Guirandou-N'Diaye, the member for the Ivory Coast, who was one of my vice-presidents. If I had any doubts my visit confirmed that the Nationalist NOC was, indeed, under considerable pressure from its government. It also confirmed that I had made a mistake in the composition of my commission, especially when I arrived there to find Cross awaiting me and wanting to accompany me on my enquiries; I declined his offer.

The delay in visiting the other side was unfortunate because the crucial session at Montevideo came in between and some members were under the impression that I was favouring mainland China. I was indeed anxious to hammer out a formula in Montevideo that brought the mainland back into the movement, and I felt increasingly that the political obstructions put up by Taiwan meant I had to demonstrate that the IOC was strong on this question and would not be manipulated. It came to light during these discussions that it was against the law in Taiwan for Taiwanese Chinese to speak or mix with those from the mainland since they were still regarded as an enemy. With such knowledge, and also knowing more of the details of a lawsuit that Taipei was now undertaking against the International Amateur Athletic Federation in London (IAAF headquarters) to annul a decision of the IAAF, I began to feel that political prevarication would continue and that the correct course was to get the People's Republic of China back in and let the Nationalists remain members, if they wished, on our terms.

To that end I persuaded my Executive Board to accept a resolution that called on the IOC "to reinstate the Chinese Olympic Committee and to maintain recognition of the Olympic Committee whose headquarters are located in Taipei." But the full session would not accept this, believing that it demoted the NOC recognised in Taipei. I wanted a resolution that did not use the word "Chinese" in reference to Taipei, for I felt that at the moment Peking would not accept such a solution and, having come so far, I was prepared to bend in the matter. But the rest of the membership would not support me and instead we passed a watery version, the second part of which referred to "the Chinese Olympic Committee located in Taipei."

The IOC also agreed that the People's Republic of China would not return to membership when Taipei was using the Nationalist flag and anthem in Olympic ceremonies that purported to indicate sovereignty over the mainland. This was indeed an absurd situation and we called on Taipei to produce a new flag, emblem, and anthem. Initially neither side accepted this solution so the matter was raised once more when the Executive Board met in Nagoya, Japan, in October 1979, which would be the last opportunity to solve the question before the Olympic year began. I had established by then that Peking's position had shifted so that there would not be objection to the title of Taipei's NOC. This I felt was a step forward, and the meeting in Nagoya agreed to call for a postal vote of all members on asking

Taipei to change its flag, emblem, and anthem. My members finally supported me and the mainland was back in the movement for the Lake Placid Winter Games, but the Nationalists were prevented from competing since they insisted on using their flag, which was no longer recognised now by the United States government. It was, in fact, a complete reversal of the Games of Montreal four years earlier, where the United States threatened to withdraw (but did not) if Taiwan did not take part (which it did not).

The Taipei NOC started a court action in Switzerland, where the IOC was situated, to protect its position in the IOC, but the case could not be proceeded with because of legal technicalities. However, when I handed over the presidency, a similar case brought by Henry Hsu was still in front of the courts. It always seemed to me odd that a member could virtually embark upon a legal action against himself but, happily, through the diplomacy of my successor, the case was dropped and the solutions found during my term of office have now been agreed by all concerned; also, members of the IOC must now resign if they wish to sue the IOC.

At the Baden-Baden congress in 1981, I was happy to see representatives of both Chinese NOCs sitting together and talking, and I hope to see their athletes competing in the same Olympic Games in the future. After all, their dispute is a political one between the two Chinese governments and, as such, requires a political solution. Sport and the Olympic Movement should not be involved.

The return of China to the Olympic fold was my most cherished dream. But the way that goal was achieved illustrated the manner in which the Olympic Movement must compromise in order to survive. There would not be so much heart searching and agonising over problems of this type if the IOC had undergone an internal restructuring of its rules so that most became principles and the remainder bye-laws and guidelines. One of the first things I did on being elected was to appoint the grand duke of Luxembourg to chair a committee to revise all the rules. This he did, and the changes are evolving today in the way he started them.

For more than eighty years there have been political prob-

lems in the Olympic Movement, but their magnitude and complexity has never been so great as through my period of office. The IOC and the international federations have to be more aware of and ready to respond to political challenge and to act in a positive manner. The problem of Chinese participation in the Olympic Movement is only one of many political issues with which the IOC has had to contend. Like many of the others it involves the East-West split.

At the time of the return of the Soviet Union to the Olympic Movement in 1951, the IOC also considered the participation of now Communist countries such as Poland, Hungary, Czechoslovakia, and Bulgaria, and since they had had Olympic committees before the Second World War there was not much problem about them. Neither was there any problem with the Federal Republic of Germany, known as West Germany. But East Germany—the German Democratic Republic—was quite a different question. It did not receive recognition for its NOC, partly because some members of the IOC were concerned about the implications of membership for a state that was not yet recognised in a large part of the Western world.

But within the IOC there was a compelling urge to get all of Germany back into the IOC. It came, in the first instance, from Ritter von Halt, the prewar president of the German NOC and a member of the IOC since 1927, who had been heavily involved in the Games of Berlin and Garmisch-Partenkirchen in 1936. After the collapse of the Third Reich, Halt was sent to a Russian concentration camp. Everything was done to liberate him and the members of his executive board who were with him. But he was detained for five years and when he returned his health was ruined. He had but one ambition to fulfil and that was the recognition of what was now the National Olympic Committee of (East) Germany. Yet there were enormous difficulties with Germany still divided in two, and there was also the problem of Berlin.

Here was an instance of the Olympic Movement, propelled only by the urge to get sportsmen together, being ahead of the United Nations. Halt, working on the project from his home in West Germany, had very close ties with Dr. Heinz Schöbel, an eminent Leipzig publisher who was president of the East German NOC and later one of my most faithful colleagues in the IOC up to the time of his death in 1980. Schöbel made several pleas for the recognition of his NOC and in 1955 in Paris he achieved success—of a kind. The IOC, by a 27 to 7 vote, agreed to provisional recognition on the understanding that it would automatically lapse if it should prove impossible to form a unified team from both Germanys. But the miracle, as it was regarded at the time, worked and a unified Germany competed in the Games of 1956. The country with the larger number of athletes chose the leader of the delegation and the hymn from Beethoven's Ninth Symphony was used as the anthem. The red, black, and yellow German flag with the Olympic rings was also used.

At the time of the 1955 decision in Paris, I, like many of my colleagues, had political reservations about encouraging a united Germany. I have many friends in both parts of Germany but also had a father killed in the First World War and a half brother killed in the Second. Having also experienced the Second World War myself, I still retain a nightmarish dread of a united Germany, fuelled by a neo-Nazi revival recommencing the search for *Lebensraum*, which led Europe into two major conflicts.

Nonetheless, I now believe that one of Brundage's outstanding triumphs was uniting, for an interim period, the two Germanys to compete jointly in 1960, 1964, and 1968. This he achieved at a time when very few countries recognised East Germany. It was unfortunate that in the late fifties, when he and his Executive Board tried to work out a similar formula for China, the history and circumstances were so different.

The German arrangement ended in 1968. With the West Germans staging the Games of 1972, they were involved in the closing ceremonies in the Mexico Games and their flag had to be raised.

If the two Germanys episode was something of which the IOC might be proud, the political manoeuvring at the Munich Games most certainly was not. After the South African question had been dealt with in 1970, the problem of apartheid in Rhodesia was raised. The IOC considered the matter in 1971 when, rather surprisingly, Rhodesia, which had renounced its British connections, agreed to compete using the Rhodesian ensign containing the Union Jack, and "God Save the Queen," as they had done at the Tokyo Games in 1964. Rhodesia arrived in Munich with a multiracial team. However, many African countries, which had agreed to the "Tokyo status quo" at a meeting with the IOC in Munich in 1971, now changed their minds, doubtless due to political pressures. For the first time since the Olympic Movement had been revived, a properly recognised NOC had its competitors withdrawn after they had been in the Olympic Village for several days. It was a humiliating decision and, in some ways, turned the key for others who would use the pressure of a boycott. But in the massacre that was soon to follow, it was a subject that quietly slipped away.

Left to right: Ronnie Delany, the film director John Ford, and the author in Honolulu on the way back from the 1956 Melbourne Games, where Delany won the gold medal in the 1,500-metre run

Being received by Pope John XXIII in St. Peter's Square prior to the 1960 Rome Games. On the right are IOC members Reginald Honey (South Africa) and, in white, Ivar Vind (Denmark).

Members of the IOC in Olympia, Greece, after the Athens session of 1954: Prince Francis Joseph II (Liechtenstein): Ritter von Halt (Germany); Lord Aberdare (Britain); Archduke Adolphe von Mecklenburg (Germany); Avery Brundage; Count Paolo Thaon di Revel (Italy), Mussolini's finance minister; the author; J. Jewett Garland (United States); unknown

At the IOC session in Madrid in 1965: Brundage; General Francisco Franco; Aleksei Romanov (USSR); the author

With Brundage at the
IOC session in Rome, 1966

(Roberto Andrei)

Meeting Empress Farah of Iran during the Tehran session in 1967: Romanov; the author; Vladimir Stoytchev (Bulgaria); the empress; Brundage

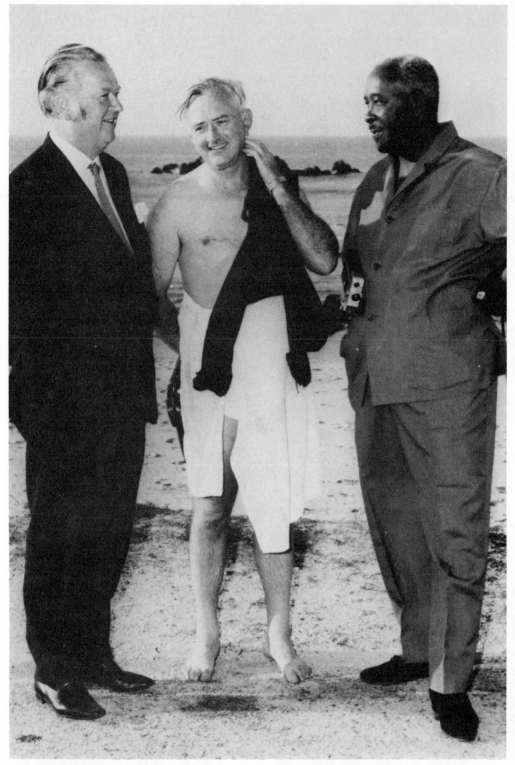

The 1967 commission to South Africa on the beach: the author; Reginald Alexander;
Sir Ade Ademola

Laying a wreath at Auschwitz after the Warsaw session of 1969. The man with the umbrella is Janusz Pieceiwiecz, an official of the Polish NOC.

Visiting Munich in 1969 after his election as vice-president of the IOC

(Olympia-Baugesellschaft MBH)

With Prince Bertil, president of the Swedish NOC, during a visit to Stockholm in 1973

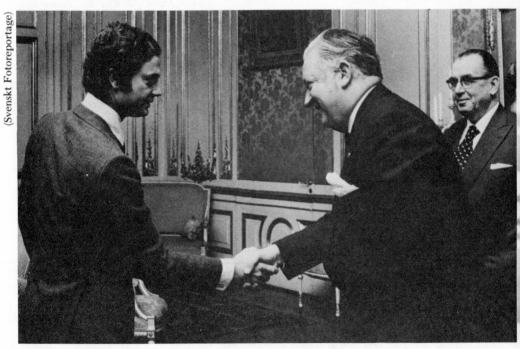

The author meeting King Carl Gustaf of Sweden in Stockholm in 1973

Addressing the congress at Varna in 1973

Visiting the "Montreal 1976" exhibition during the 1974 IOC session in Vienna:
James Worrall (Canada); Roger Rousseau, president of the Montreal organising committee; the author; Rudolf Nemetschke (Austria); Mohammed Mzali (Tunisia)

A briefing session in Moscow in 1976 on the Olympic structures proposed by the organising committee for the 1980 Games

Queen Elizabeth and the author at the opening of the 1976 Montreal Games

The opening of the IOC session in Athens in 1978, at the Acropolis. On the author's right are Lady Killanin; Greek President Constantine Tsatsos; Mme. Tsatsos

Announcing that Los Angeles had been awarded the 1984 Games, at the Athens session of 1978. *Front:* Mzali; Samaranch; the author; Padilha. *Back:* Vitaly Smirnov (USSR); Count de Beaumont (France); Arpad Csanadi (Hungary); Worrall—all members of the Executive Board

At Lake Placid for the World Skating Championships in 1978, with the late Ronald McKenzie of the Lake Placid organising committee

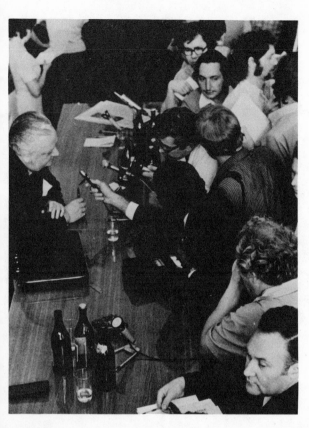

The author giving radio interviews following a 1979 press conference in Yugoslavia

In discussion with President Jimmy Carter at the White House in 1980. The empty seat was for National Security Adviser Zbigniew Brzezinski, who arrived later.

At the Kremlin in 1980: Monique Berlioux, the IOC director; Smirnov; the author; an interpreter; President Leonid Brezhnev; Ignati Novikov of the organising committee; Brezhnev's adviser Blatov

Discussions at the Kremlin. On Brezhnev's left are Novikov; Blatov; Smirnov. Berlioux is on the author's right.

With Novikov during the opening ceremony

The opening of the Olympic Games in Moscow, July 19, 1980. The author is presenting the mayor of Moscow, Vladimir Promislov, with the Olympic flag. The two athletes are Canadians who had brought the flag from Montreal.

The IOC Executive Board outside the IOC headquarters at the Château de Vidy in Lausanne in 1979: Lance Cross (New Zealand); Masaji Kiyokawa (Japan); Csanadi; Smirnov; Padilha; the author; Mzali; Berlioux; Louis Guirandou-N'Diaye (Ivory Coast); Beaumont

At the Baden-Baden congress of 1981, with Exeter (*seated*) during the latter's last attendance and Grand Duke Jean of Luxembourg

President Samaranch presents the author with the Olympic Order (Gold) at the Baden-Baden congress.

The author presents a Waterford crystal globe to Berlioux in Dublin in 1981.

Looking back in Dublin—Lord Killanin in his study

Oh, God! Oh, Montreal!

The Montreal years, from the time the Canadian city was awarded the Games to their opening in 1976, were agonising ones for the movement and for me. I don't know whether Montreal or Moscow was more damaging to the Olympic concept, but my wife believes that the coronary I suffered in 1977 was partly due to the increasing burden of problems I had to face during 1975 and 1976.

The Games of Montreal became synonymous with Jean Drapeau, the flamboyant mayor of the city. Drapeau cut a dapper figure. He was a small man of sober dress, with a neatly trimmed moustache. Inspired by the Olympic ideal after visiting the IOC headquarters in Lausanne in the late fifties, he developed a sincere interest in the movement and first made an impression in Olympic circles in 1966, when he led Montreal's bid for the Games of 1972, which went to Munich. Even there his sharp business aptitude was noticed, for he offered free accommodation in the Olympic Village for all competitors, something no other Olympic city had included in its hospitality. He returned in 1970 to ask the IOC to give his city the Games of 1976.

Drapeau seemed to be running a one-man campaign. In the foyer and public rooms he would approach people in the politest possible terms. "Sir, may I talk to you about Montreal" was delivered in English rich with a French accent. His presentation was for modest Games, set forward in simple terms with a model of some of the proposed sites, which included a main stadium that looked neat and uncomplicated. Drapeau also spoke much about "auto-financement" (self-financing), which meant the Games could fund themselves. This was not to be the case, although it was the policy subsequently expounded and is being implemented by Los Angeles.

There is always high drama when the announcement of the winning bid is made, and this session in Amsterdam had more than its share. When Brundage stood on the stage of the conference centre and opened the envelope containing the result, the three principals, the mayors of Montreal, Los Angeles, and Moscow, were seated in the front row. On the first count Brundage announced Moscow was ahead, but without an overall majority, and before he could get out his next sentence with the final result, Tass, the Soviet news agency, had flashed a message round the world that Moscow had won. Perhaps not surprisingly, a Pan-American bloc of seventeen votes, which on the first count went to Los Angeles, all moved it appeared to Montreal, though one cannot be sure of course in a secret ballot. With Montreal's victory, there were tears in abundance from that city's hostesses in their vivid red dresses. Meanwhile Mayor Promislov of Moscow had walked out, not to be seen again in Amsterdam. The Russians had clearly believed that they were going to be awarded the Games.

Drapeau then made his way to the press room telephones to call up a leading chef from Montreal and put into operation a well-laid plan. A plane left the Quebec city that night loaded with food, and twenty-four hours later seven hundred people sat down to a home-style Montreal dinner in the banqueting hall of the Amsterdam Hilton. There were thirty-two different kinds of food, though Montreal would not, of course, claim the origin of every one. It was a great occasion but, on reflection, it was the beginning of much unnecessary expense, which brought the cost of the Montreal Games to over one billion dollars.

My worries began almost as soon as I became president two years later. There had been long delays in setting up the organising committee in Montreal, and when I went there late in 1972 work had already fallen behind. I asked to see the budget. Drapeau, who had taken charge, was driving me round the possible sites for the events and alternatives for the Olympic

Village, press centre, and other essential parts of an Olympic city. He kept on saying, "I have my budget here." "Here" consisted of a foolscap envelope that could only have contained a few figures. After the Games the Quebec government set up a judicial commission under Justice Malouf to enquire into the financing of the Games. The resulting report showed there had been no realistic budgeting, but an open-ended account.

While I always found Drapeau an honest man, his personality dominated the whole operation when the organisation should have been left to those appointed to the job. Drapeau had picked an ambassador to organise Expo 67 in Montreal and sought a person of similar diplomatic and commercial experience, with a knowledge of sport, as president of the Montreal Olympic organising committee, which was technically responsible to the Canadian NOC although the city had taken charge. Roger Rousseau, who had been in the commercial department of Canada's Foreign Service and had a low golf handicap, seemed to fit the requirements and was appointed. But with Rousseau's diplomatic background, training in traditional methods of running government, and conformity to discipline, Drapeau's unorthodox methods were bound to bring clashes. In fact, at times their relationship was barely tolerable.

As an example of Drapeau's mercurial nature, some have pointed to his switch from a small, orthodox stadium to one with two tiers and a retractable roof. But in all fairness he did this because the Canadian winter called for a construction that kept out the weather. A complete indoor stadium, such as the Astrodome in Houston, would have been unacceptable for the major Olympic sport of track and field, and for American football, one of the sports for which Drapeau wanted to use the stadium after the Games. In planning Olympic facilities, organising committees must look beyond the Games themselves to ensure that the sports infrastructure can be used by the city. That is what Drapeau did.

A decision with more serious repercussions was Drapeau's choice of a Paris architect, Roger Taillibert, to design the stadium. Among his many outstanding works, Taillibert had designed the Parc des Princes in Paris. He based his design for the Montreal stadium on that one. Apart from the fact that he was three thousand miles away from the site, there was also national jealousy that a Canadian had not been chosen for this most prestigious task. In addition, Taillibert was able to work in absolute freedom. If cost limitations had been set, the choice of design would have been subject to this restriction.

Once the construction was underway, there were labour problems compounded by the fact that certain parts of the construction, involving steel components, could not be completed before winter. Thus, in the deep subzero temperatures that Montreal suffers, the work had to be delayed until the following spring. Anxiety spread within the IOC, which was hardly allayed by Drapeau's reports to the Executive Board and the full IOC. He once appeared with a series of multicoloured cards showing just how and when all the work was to be done and completed. The board was still left worrying about the reaction of the trade unions, which were being asked to bend all kinds of agreements to get installations finished, and the costs to be borne ultimately by the taxpayers of Montreal and Quebec. This is not what the members of the IOC had voted for at Amsterdam.

James Worrall, the IOC member for Canada and a lawyer in Toronto, was keeping me fully informed of Drapeau's progress and by the middle of 1975 I feared that Montreal was not going to be completed in time for the Games. I therefore decided that we should make some contingency plans for an alternative site. There were plenty of suggestions being made as to what we should do. One was to postpone the Games, but this did not take into account the Olympic rules, the world's sporting calendar, or the time scale of training to which potential Olympic sportsmen gear themselves. This last factor was uppermost in my mind. Young people all over the world were preparing for Olympic competition. When it came down to it, the venue was not important, but the challenge for the medal was. Also, it would have been impossible at short notice to transfer the whole Games to another city; the facilities might have been available but we could never have found all the necessary accommodation for competitors, officials, reporters, and, of course, spectators, not to mention transferring the television arrangements. To this end Worrall and the IOC vice-presidents held several secret meetings at an airport hotel in Amsterdam on preliminary plans for an alternative. There were offers to stage the Games in Mexico and a supposed one from Munich. I did not go out of my way to discourage any of these because they provided a publicity smokescreen for my own scheme.

My plan was to hold as many events, if not all the twenty-one sports of the programme, at venues in northern West Germany, which is well equipped with the sports facilities we needed. Düsseldorf has a large athletic stadium and there are excellent rowing facilities at Duisburg and Essen, as well as a choice of swimming pools and plenty of indoor arenas to cope with gymnastics, judo, wrestling, and the other indoor events. Soccer would not have presented any problems because the sport is highly popular in Germany. There were times when I felt we would need these facilities and others when the surge of good news from Montreal lifted our spirits.

The critical time was the autumn of 1975. Much construction still needed to be done, yet the onset of the Canadian winter restricted the work. It was early in October that I heard the Quebec government intended to take over the construction board, appointing to it Dr. Victor Goldbloom, the provincial minister of the environment and municipal affairs. At first I sighed in the belief that here was just another man to join in the squabble, and that the intervention of the Quebec government would only add to the bureaucracy. I was wrong, and in the year after the Montreal Games when one could reflect on the tangle and put a sharper perspective to all events, I felt that without Goldbloom the Games would not have taken place.

He set up an office in Montreal, took time to absorb all the facts of the situation, and believed that, whatever happened, Montreal, Quebec, and Canada had a responsibility to the competitors around the world to ensure that the Games started on time in adequate facilities, and never mind the fripperies. He brought me immense support for, from early December 1975 until almost the start of the Games in the summer of 1976, he would telephone me in Dublin at least once a week with a detailed progress report. Whenever I felt that Rousseau or Drapeau was passing the buck, I could, without compunction, go straight to Goldbloom.

By the time of the Executive Board meeting at Innsbruck in February 1976, we were to have the final detailed reports of the Montreal organising committee. I called for a guarantee that all twenty-one sports on the summer programme would take place as scheduled. In the preparation for those meetings there was need for much communication between the IOC and the organising committee. It was, therefore, infuriating to ring up Rousseau for some important information, probably as a result of requests from an international federation, to find that he was away on a fishing holiday. He preferred the social side of being president of an organising committee, and I was furious when, in Innsbruck, I discovered that Rousseau would be arriving a day late because he was going to a ball in Germany on the way. Admittedly it was to promote the Games, but I had turned down an invitation because of the crisis and the organisers knew of my reasons; it must have been embarrassing for them to have the man who should have been at the helm in Montreal being wined and dined, while I waited for him, tapping my fingers impatiently, in Innsbruck.

After many phone calls I felt I knew Goldbloom well, so it was a surprise when I met him and found myself confronted with a democratic Napoleon. Like Drapeau, he was short in stature, with very active eyes. By profession a paediatrician, he was a remarkable troubleshooter and helped restore some of the confidence when he reported to the IOC. But I still had my doubts, with the many construction strikes and even one in the post office, which meant important mail had to be sent to the United States and carried across the border by courier.

As I look back, I realise how much Goldbloom contributed towards saving the Games. When one official was saying that there would be no construction work over Christmas and another equally important one was saying there would, I could get Goldbloom to establish the facts and impel him to stop people making contradictory statements that worried the Olympic world.

One aspect he could not control, however, was the escalating costs. For example, the stadium was constructed on a ring of what I call G concrete stands, since they shaped the letter G. In normal building construction of this kind, a railway carrying a crane would be laid on the inside of the proposed G sitings, and the crane would move round hauling into place the parts that made up the G and linking them all together to form the shell of the stadium. That alone is an expensive operation. But, in this instance, there was not time for the leisurely shunting of a crane on a railway line. Many of them had to be hired from all over North America, so that each G virtually had its own crane.

A colleague of mine was in Montreal just eighty days before the Games began and he came back with a dismal picture. He was allowed to clamber up inside one of those G constructions to its uppermost point and peer down on the infield, where there was no track, but there were eighty lorries and other vehicles. Even though hundreds of men were at work he could not envisage a complete stadium. Of course the stadium was not finished—that curved sweep of a tower from which the retractable roof was to be suspended had long been abandoned—but the arena was ready for the athletes, the grass having been grown elsewhere and resodded in the stadium.

While building the main stadium was a race in itself, the

height of Montreal's folly concerned the Olympic Village. It was part of the city's agreement with the IOC in 1970 to provide a village in which the athletes, by tradition, live. In 1974, two years before the Games, the city passed over the responsibility to the organising committee, which could not find any one developer to build accommodation. When the organising committee presented its report to the IOC session in Vienna in 1974, there was still no real proposal. In a room of their hotel the delegation put together the idea of forming their own company to build the Village.

Drapeau was fascinated by the installations of the Baie des Anges marina on the outskirts of Nice, France. For the South of France this pyramid project of living accommodation was utterly in complement with the climate, but transferring the idea to one of the coldest inhabited areas of North America seemed ludicrous. The project was to have cost nine million dollars; this escalated to beyond seventy million.

Galloping inflation, strikes, work stoppages, the saturation of the construction market at the time—these were contributory conditions to the catastrophe that almost overtook Montreal. But the blame falls heavily upon Drapeau. The organising committee was slow in appointing project managers, a task the Malouf commission of enquiry said was that of the mayor: "Not only was he entirely lacking in aptitudes and knowledge required for this role, but also, as a politician and first magistrate of the city, he should have avoided placing himself in this position." For a man whose vision only was to make Montreal a magnet for the world, as he did with Expo 67 and then the Olympic Games, it was a harsh condemnation. The commission's report and a study of Montreal's organisation are essential reading for any prospective Olympic Games host city.

At a point in the spring of 1975 when it seemed that the celebration in Montreal would actually take place, I became concerned about plans for the opening ceremony, in which the head of state of the host nation, in this instance Queen Elizabeth, would normally take part. In Canada, with rivalries of race and language much to the fore at the time and various factions on the lookout for a platform on which to stage some demonstration, the question of whether the queen would be asked to perform the opening ceremony had not been broached, but I was informed that the governor-general, Jules Léger, as the head of state's representative, was to undertake the task. I was assured several times by the Canadian authorities that he was their choice. I was therefore surprised to hear on the car radio, when driving with James Worrall from Toronto to Montreal on April 25, 1975, that the Games were to be opened by the queen; and if I was surprised, Mayor Drapeau was alarmed. When I returned to Europe I got in touch with Buckingham Palace for formal confirmation of the news and was told that "Her Majesty's prime minister had advised her to open the Games." My immediate reaction was "What the devil has this to do with Harold Wilson?" but then I realised, of course, that the prime minister in question was that of Canada, Pierre Trudeau. On a visit to London he had decided, on his own judgement apparently, to invite her to perform the opening.

She was, in fact, due to arrive in Canada on the royal yacht *Britannia* a few days prior to the beginning of the Games with other members of her family. Prince Philip is president of the International Equestrian Federation (FEI) and, like all other presidents of sports on the Olympic programme, has a busy time during the Games.

This, of course, produced new problems of security and protocol, and one of the most delicate points was the language in which she would declare open the Games. At first it was decided that English would be used, but this clearly produced an unfavourable reaction from the French-speaking majority in Quebec, so a change to French was made on the grounds that French takes precedence over English in the Olympic Movement.

There was to be a separate opening ceremony at the yachting centre in Kingston, Ontario, and at that rehearsal my stand-in spoke French; a cable came swiftly from the Ontario authorities to the effect that if I went there and spoke French I should be run out of Kingston. When the day came, I delivered the main part of my speech in English with a few words of French at the end—and escaped with my skin.

Some of the longest minutes of my life were those spent waiting with the queen to enter the stadium in Montreal for the opening of the Games. She looked, as she always does on such occasions, serene and calm, though I am sure she felt apprehensive. I certainly did. In fact all fears were groundless, for the queen received a tremendous ovation—I think for the stunning pink coat, dress, and hat that she wore, which marked her out among the soberly dressed IOC, NOC, and IF heads.

The success of the splendid opening ceremony was for me a monumental relief. Hardly had the worries of whether we would have a stadium in which to open the Games subsided than two other problems of a political nature loomed: the exclusion of Taiwan from the Games by the Canadian authorities, and the boycott by the African countries among others.

When a city applies for the Games, the International Olympic Committee requires the support and certain undertakings of both the city and the country. In the instance of Canada an undertaking was asked for, and given, that all national Olympic committees would be allowed to enter Canada to take part in the Games. The only question remotely related to Taiwan's participation was discussed twelve months before the Games with Mitchell Sharp, an official at the Department of External Affairs in Ottawa, who enquired as to the position of the mainland Chinese, with whom there had been discussions about a return to the Olympic Movement. There was, though, no indication that Taiwan would be excluded; that news did not reach me until the end of May 1976. Not to allow the Taiwanese into the country was a breach of the Canadian government's agreement. I informed the Canadian Department of External Affairs, through the organising committee, but there was no retraction. However, the organising committee had issued Taiwan's team Olympic identity cards, which permitted entry into Canada, according to the rules, and the chairman of the committee was, of course, Rousseau, a seconded Foreign Service officer.

When I and my members arrived in Montreal for the Executive Board meeting and the IOC session that are always held just before the Games are opened, the problem had become further complicated because some of the Taiwanese with American passports were already in the country preparing for the yachting events at Kingston. Henry Hsu, the IOC member, arrived on a Hong Kong identity card. With the support of my board I began to work on a compromise. I had several telephone discussions with Trudeau, and told him that he was not conforming to the guarantees the Canadian government had given in 1970; eventually he yielded on two counts and agreed that Taiwan's team could take part, using their national flag and anthem but not the name "Republic of China." I think that Taiwan's officials should have accepted this compromise for the sake of their competitors.

Canada was under pressure from mainland China to have Taiwan excluded. Canada had recently resumed diplomatic relations with the People's Republic, and part of the latter's demands for returning to the Games was that since she controlled Taiwan (which of course she did not), countries having diplomatic relations with the mainland should not separately recognise Taiwan. This really was a problem for the politicians but, as with so many events, it found its way into the Olympic arena. There were suggestions at the time that Trudeau was under considerable pressure from the Chinese because of his grain contracts, but I learned later that this was a misconception.

This was, again, breaking our own rules, but at that eleventh hour my only concern was to get Taiwan's athletes, who had like every other Olympic sportsman been preparing so long, into the arenas. If the Canadians were playing politics, then so too were the Taiwanese, for when the plan was put to their NOC, Richard Ting, one of their representatives, rejected it in an aggressive tone and I had to rebuke him for his attitude. On top of that the United States fired a broadside when the USOC president, Phil Krumm, announced that if Taiwan competed his country would withdraw; again the United States was reviving its relationship with the mainland of China, but continued the recognition of Taiwan, which policy the USOC was instructed to follow.

Krumm used a powerful weapon with his threat. Under the terms of the television agreement with ABC, the American network that had paid a considerable sum for the rights, if no American team took part the contract could be invalid. That clause was subsequently withdrawn from future contracts so perhaps I have something to thank Krumm for, since he at least drew attention to a dangerous loophole in the television contract. However, with the Taiwanese rejecting the compromise to which Trudeau agreed, Krumm's bark was not followed by a bite.

Some people pressed me to allow the Taiwanese athletes to take part in the opening ceremony, since this was on Olympic territory, not Canadian, but I feared that there might have been demonstrations against the authorities, who would surely have tried to stop them reaching the arena. Under no circumstances was I going to encourage violence.

The more serious problem of those July days was the threat, which eventually materialised, of withdrawal from the Games by the African countries. As so often happens in internationalism, a string of events, mostly unforeseen, locked together to present the IOC with a challenge to which it could not bow. Prime Minister Robert Muldoon had won an election in New Zealand early in the year in which freedom for rugby players to go where they pleased was a fairly strong point. Soon after that a rugby tour to South Africa by New Zealand was arranged, which brought protests from other African nations. Many said they would not take part in the Montreal Games if New Zealand was allowed to compete. The events were compounded by the recent riots in Soweto, the black township on the outskirts of Johannesburg, in which many people were killed.

Abraham Ordia and Jean-Claude Ganga, the leaders of the African NOCs through the SCSA, came to see me in my hotel suite in Montreal. Ganga was the more intelligent and easier to deal with; Ordia, through his English education, had acquired the trappings of diplomacy but lacked Ganga's vitality.

Ordia, I think, must have known that there was little hope of New Zealand's being thrown out, for his country's airline, Nigeria Airways, kept a plane in Montreal ready to take home the athletes while our talks continued. The final withdrawal came twenty-four hours before the Games were due to start and there were tearful scenes of African competitors in their new uniforms packing their bags and going home. Few even had time to buy souvenirs, though in view of the bitter circumstances I wonder whether they wanted any mementoes of Montreal or

DAILY MAIL — JULY 20, 1976.

the Olympic Games. I cursed the politicians for their interference with sport.

At the opening ceremony I sat with the queen, who, like thousands of others in the stadium, showed her anxiety and sadness at the blank spaces in the team parade. With her, I was trying to discover which of the African and other delegations were missing or present.

The Games were clouded by a number of minor incidents created by the Ukrainian émigré population, which is strong in the north of Montreal. Demonstrations, including the burning of a Soviet flag outside the Village, were dealt with rapidly by the Canadian police.

The question of the withdrawal of teams was discussed the following year at the IOC Executive Board meeting in Barcelona. Twenty-two teams had not appeared, but some of these had been unable to come because they did not have either sufficient funds or competitors of Olympic standard. There was a feeling that those countries that withdrew for political reasons should be sanctioned, but it was a measure that would not affect the politicians. A new rule was passed so that an NOC that had entered athletes for competitions could not withdraw them except on grounds of health, and this was designed to dissuade countries carrying their demonstrations into the Olympic arena where, for instance, an African runner might refuse to appear in the same heat as a New Zealander. Perhaps the IOC was weak not to sanction those who withdrew for political reasons. Another precedent had been set. There was, at one point, a mild Soviet threat to withdraw from the Games because one of their swimmers had disappeared. They believed he had sought political asylum in the United States, but in fact it appears he sought asylum in the arms of a lady he had met there. He returned in due course to his team and calm was restored.

The abiding memory of Montreal must be the escalating costs upon which a check was put far too late and which, in fact, could not be properly controlled because of the commitment to a date of readiness. The story tarnished the reputation of the Olympic Movement and undoubtedly frightened potential hosts, who believed that it was no longer possible to stage the Games at reasonable cost.

The closing ceremony had its usual jovial side, a feeling that a lot of people had found new friends and that, after all, Moscow and 1980 were not far off. The closing, too, brought a new, novel demonstration. In the Games of Mexico in 1968 there were the Black Power demonstrators; four years later in Munich a flabby-looking individual trotted into the arena and had many people believing he was the first marathon runner; and Montreal had its streaker. I noticed this naked man dancing in a circle of white-clad ladies and wondered how on earth, without an identity card, he had managed to get through the security. There seemed no great haste to cover the exposure and one of the primmer Canadians sitting next to me continually tried to divert my attention from the incident. The streaker was arrested, charged, and fined a small sum for his contribution to Olympic history.

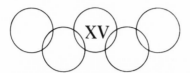

Protocol and Ceremonial

Pomp and ceremony, a mixture of ritual and religion in the opening ceremony and the presentation of the medals, lift the Olympic Games above other sporting festivals. Coubertin saw the need for them and drew on Hellenic religion and Dr. Thomas Arnold's hearty Christianity, blending these for the Olympic arena. Those who decry this part of the Games must remember that the largest single audience on television is for the opening and closing ceremonies. This has something to do with the fact that the broadcasters now produce their own spectacular section of the opening ceremony, but in addition this modern world warped by corruption, violence, and immorality is eager to see those involved in any event—sporting, cultural, or otherwise—express faith in what they are doing.

Many people say that the opening ceremony is hypocritical. "They're all professionals" is the sort of sweeping statement that achieves misplaced popularity. The IOC does not have officials who could screen every competitor to make sure she or he is being honest in taking the oath. Even today, with many eligibility rules relaxed, there are those who are dishonest; my hope is that having taken part in the Games and gone on to live their lives, they will look back on the Olympic experience as having given them and perhaps their children a new attitude towards life. The only part of Olympic ceremonial that raises my hackles is the overt nationalism; the national flags and anthems should be dispensed with.

Many people imagine that all these ceremonies originated with the first Games in 1896. In fact, many are of a later date, like the Olympic Villages themselves, and have evolved in the same way.

The emblem of the entwined rings, which Coubertin patterned on one found in ancient Greece, was not used until the celebration at Antwerp in 1920 and the flag presented by the Belgian city then is now handed on at each opening ceremony of the Games from one mayor to the next for safekeeping; it has become part of the ceremonial. The rings are symbols of the five continents and include the blue, yellow, black, green, and red colours found in most national flags—a neutral motif representing the world. Modifications are taking place all the time, some by outside forces such as television, but at the Lake Placid session there was a significant shift in the control of these matters when the question of protocol was moved from the main rules to the bye-laws. This means that changes can now be achieved through a simple majority vote rather than the two-thirds majority previously required.

The protocol for the sessions of the IOC and for the Games themselves—where it is limited to regulating the opening ceremony, the awarding of medals, and the closing ceremony—is worth examining in detail. The procedure for the IOC meetings is governed by instructions, included in the charter, which cover such administrative matters as the issuing of invitations, accommodation, the layout of conference rooms, receptions, the agenda, rules for debate, and so on. Other instructions cover simultaneous translation, the secretariat, and the responsibilities of the IOC and the organising committees, as well as facilities for the media.

The head of state—or whomever he delegates if he cannot attend—performs the opening ceremony at the session preceding the Games. On this occasion the speakers are the head of state, the president of the host NOC, and the president of the IOC. Nobody else is permitted to speak and, as president of the IOC, I usually made this an occasion for a policy speech and an introduction to the main points that would be covered in the ensuing session.

The president of the NOC usually makes a speech of welcome. In the past he was followed by the president of the IOC, who then asked the head of state to open the session. Some heads of state have spoken excellently and to the point. Others have pontificated at length about Olympic principles, frequently producing no more than a string of platitudes. In Madrid in 1965, General Francisco Franco confined himself simply to declaring the session open. Though this order of speakers had never been laid down, it had become traditional. However, after the vitriolic speech made by U.S. Secretary of State Cyrus Vance at Lake Placid (a matter I deal with in Chapter XX), it was realised that the traditional order must be changed, so now the president of the IOC always speaks last in order to correct any mistakes and have the last word. The first time the new procedure was tried was when, taking the floor after the representative of the head of state, I made the initial welcome and opening speech at the session at Moscow. This saved time and set the tone of our subsequent discussions.

The head of state on these occasions has been regarded as apolitical and this was a valid supposition in the days when much of the world was ruled by monarchs. But now, with the increasing number of politically nominated or elected presidents, such as the presidents of the United States and France, the risk that the privilege of opening sessions will be used for political or chauvinistic purposes has greatly increased. The new rule that the president of the IOC shall speak last is thus a safeguard.

It would be far better in the future if both the Games and the session were opened by the president of the IOC—whose organisation is responsible for them—in the presence of the head of state. This was further emphasised by the problem faced at Moscow, where competitors, without wishing to show any disrespect to the head of state by not saluting him as instructed in the regulations, nevertheless felt in conscience that they would be showing political agreement if they paid him this normal courtesy. It has never been compulsory to parade at the opening of the Games, although it has been customary; moreover, absence for political reasons is contrary to Olympic principles.

The opening of the session is punctuated by music and songs, which provide an opportunity for the display of national talents and fulfil the IOC aim of combining culture with sport.

The Olympic hymn has always formed part of the ceremonial, and I am pleased that the original hymn has not been changed in spite of efforts towards this end over the years. The music was composed by Spyros Samaras for the first modern Games in Athens. All attempts at finding a new one failed and in 1958 Samaras's composition was adopted as the official Olympic hymn. It is very moving, especially when performed, as it usually is, by a good orchestra and choir. Whatever else in the Olympic Movement and protocol may need changing, the hymn should be left alone. It is already a tradition.

The high ceremonial point of the opening ceremony of the Games is the arrival of the flame. This is, relatively speaking, an innovation. The flame, a symbol of striving for perfection and victory, was a suggestion by the IOC member for Germany, Theodore Lewald, before the Games in 1928 at Amsterdam. He suggested that the flame be lit in Olympia, Greece, and carried to the Games. The idea was accepted, but in Amsterdam the relay did not take place though the flame burned in the stadium. It was not until the Berlin Games of 1936 that the full ceremony beginning in Olympia was carried out, and it was later adopted for the Winter Games. I think this is an important part of the educational work that the IOC must develop. The organisation of the flame relay needs a tremendous amount of work and brings to many people, particularly the young, a close link with the Games.

The medal ceremony has remained largely unchanged. It has retained that moment when the focus is turned upon the victor, who is presented not only with the prize but a memory that will be treasured for life. I think that some of my happiest Olympic recollections are of those occasions when, offstage at the edge of the arena and out of sight, I have exchanged a few informal words with the medallists.

Lake Placid, which unhappily did not make many contributions to Olympic advancement, provided one excellent idea that initially went wrong. It was decided that the medal ceremonies should take place between the day and evening competitions on a lake close to the centre of the town. It was a splendid opportunity for the local people and others who might not have tickets for the venues to see the Olympic champions close at hand. But on the first night the flagpoles had not been erected and, having waited for them to be rushed to the lake, we then found that the holes in the ice were not the correct size. This is the price of giving the Games to a small town—a quaint idea that is impractical. Finally, I told the *chef de protocole* to go ahead without the flags and the hostess came forward with the first medal. Then it slipped from the smooth cushion and I failed to catch it, but the headline writers were quick to jump and at breakfast the following morning I read, KILLANIN DROPS A CLANGER.

There are, too, awards for those who are not necessarily competitors. There were in the past various trophies and cups presented by good people who wanted the recognition of individuals and institutions involved in the Olympic Movement. There had been much pressure to change this system, and in 1974 I was successful in getting the IOC to institute the Olympic Order. This has grades of gold, silver, and bronze. The gold was originally reserved for former presidents of the IOC; the silver is presented to former presidents of international federations and national Olympic committees; the bronze goes to a more broadly based group, including competitors as well as administrators and supporters.

The Council of the Order is under the chancellorship of the president of the IOC, who is supported by three vice-presidents and the *chef de protocole*. An active member of the IOC may not be admitted to the order. Nominations may be received for each grade in annual quotas proposed by the council and finally decided by the Executive Board. At the time of expiration of my term of office as president, I admit I used this as a sort of Dissolution Honours List and made the largest number of awards so far. When I did this I had not realised that Lord Exeter was going to propose from the floor that I should be the second recipient of the gold medal of the Olympic Order, previously only awarded posthumously, in 1975, to Avery Brundage. Thus I was in the position of being the only living recipient of the highest grade of the order that I myself had inaugurated.

The only other award now presented annually is the Olympic Cup, which remains reserved for institutions or associations with a general reputation for merit and integrity that have contributed substantially to the development of the Olympic Movement.

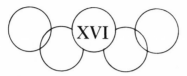

Money, Money, Money

$\mathbf{I}$s the price too high? The world takes time off from its troubles and labours every four years to watch the youthful and the not so youthful participating in the greatest of all festivals of sport. Over a billion television viewers watched the events in Montreal. That figure, with China back in the movement, probably will double for the 1984 Games in Los Angeles. But the colour and excitement of winning and losing, breaking world records, and achieving new performances entails high costs. In fact, the publicity that the Games gets each four years usually relates either to finance or to politics.

Coubertin conceived the Olympic Movement as built on amateurism, and applied that criterion to all aspects of the Games, not just to the competitors. He would never have envisaged that finance would loom so large, for in the late nineteenth century, grand patronage could take care of the grand ideas that he formulated. There were hiccups in the preparations for the first Games in Athens in 1896 and it required a private benefactor, Georgis Averoff, who donated 920,000 drachmas, to finance the rebuilding of the marble Panathenaic stadium.

The postwar period of the Games, beginning with London in 1948, can be divided into two sections: improvisation and expansion. Two years after the war Olympic competitors were glad to make do with what utility London had to offer, four years later Helsinki improvised too around its marvellous athletic stadium, and in Melbourne in 1956 the Australians made

149

temporary conversions. But growth was abroad, and once television brought the Games to more people, from Rome and Squaw Valley in 1960, the number of events and competitors began to increase. If the demands that the IOC appeared to be making in requirements from those wishing to stage the Games seemed unrealistic, there are now several cities around the world benefiting from the infrastructure the Games brought.

Tokyo built new city highways and a monorail from the airport for the Games. It sounded as though the Olympic Games demanded these requirements; they did not, but Tokyo needed these installations and achieved them so much more quickly because of the Games.

Before the 1972 Munich Games there was criticism about the extravagance in construction of the main stadium, especially of the translucent roof, which hung like a tent and which someone said would fall down within a few years. Yet it is still in its original position. That style of roof helped the broadcasters, since with a normal stand there would have been a shadow cutting across the arena, which would create difficulties in television presentation. The Olympic Village was very empty for several years after the Games. But that was some years ago and today the Olympia Park area is a thriving limb of Munich. Where the athletes lounged in their Village grounds there is a multiplicity of tennis courts fully used, and the main indoor hall is used over two hundred days per year. Munich might have built these facilities without being awarded the Games, but it would have taken a much longer time.

In Montreal, where indeed there was enormous waste, the facilities are well used, but I regret that the taxpayers are still footing the bill. The IOC must ensure that a closer watch is maintained on organising committees in the future.

The full cost of the Moscow Games will probably never be known, but as far as actual sporting facilities and amenities were concerned, the Games doubtless could have been put on the day after the venue was announced, such is the multitude of purpose-built halls, stadiums, soccer fields, and running tracks spread throughout that massive city. The Lenin Stadium was renovated and the capacity was *reduced* to one hundred thousand for greater comfort.

The one installation that always caused me worries was the facility for rowing and canoeing, which was very expensive and had restricted use. I am afraid that the demands of Thomas Keller, the president of the rowing federation, seeking perfection, have been pitched very high.

At the Games of Rome the rowing was held on a lake below Castel Gandolfo, the summer residence of the pope. I remember the competition well. My wife was not with me at those Games but I took our eldest son, Redmond, then aged twelve. He was introduced to Pope John XXIII and was looking at one of the races from a window of the castle. As he watched the oarsmen striving for victory, the pope said to him, "Remember, not only sport; read books." I think the advice was taken.

Since then, rowing courses to accommodate races over 2,000 metres have been constructed for each set of Games at considerable cost. Trying to arrange the location to avoid wind giving some competitors an advantage is difficult, if not impossible. Even at the magnificent Munich course, Keller delayed the finals for a while because wind was disturbing the water in one or two of the lanes but not the others. Having gone to such an enormous cost to produce fair competition, the organising committee must have wondered, as they waited for the wind to die down, whether their money had been properly spent. I am glad to see that rowing returns to a natural lake at the Games in 1984, although a basin was promised in the original Los Angeles bid in Athens.

Some of the money generated by television helps to provide these facilities and governments have helped in subsidising competitors. This happened in Munich, where the federal government was interested in the Third World, and many of the NOCs threatening to walk out on the Games because of the appearance of the Rhodesian team, had, in fact, been subsidised at least in part by the Germans to be present in Munich. Nothing of this sort happened in Montreal, but the Soviets, in their efforts to influence the maximum number of NOCs before the Moscow Olympics, visited certain Third World countries making very generous offers, sometimes publicly, sometimes privately, long before they invaded Afghanistan.

While for administrative reasons the Games must be given

to a city, that city may now, with the approval of the IOC, share the Games with others. It must be easy for participants to move rapidly to their places of competition, and the same applies for spectators and officials, while the competitors and team officials must be able to return to a main village. Special arrangements have always had to be made for sports that must be practised far away from the main Games city. You cannot bring the sea to the centre of Europe or the centre of the Soviet Union, and therefore must take the sailing competitions to the sea. At the Munich Games the yachting events were held in Kiel; at the Games in Moscow they took place in Tallinn in Estonia. Indeed, I consider it feasible for a group of neighbouring countries to be awarded the Olympic Games, but here the problem becomes political since it involves the question of guarantee of free access from all the governments concerned. All the same, why should there not be a Benelux Olympic Games, Games in the geographic British Isles, or Scandinavian Games? This idea could be even more applicable to the emerging and developing countries in Africa, Asia, and Central America, although in some of them communications are still extremely difficult and, indeed, primitive.

During the Games at Montreal, Prime Minister (later President) Constantine Karamanlis of Greece wrote to me suggesting there should be a permanent site for the Games in his country. From the outset I was never a supporter of this idea, but I appointed a committee of enquiry.

The scheme was found to be so impractical that there was no report on the question. Yet the subject was revived again by Karamanlis during the crisis of 1980. The emotion surrounding the months in the run-up to Moscow made the idea sound more attractive. But the arguments against the idea are manifold. Firstly, the founder of the Games wanted to spread them around the world. On the sporting side, it would be unfair that some competitors would always have to compete outside of their time zone.

If you are going to have a permanent site, then it needs to be in a country of absolute stability. Many international organisations have chosen Switzerland as their headquarters, and I could not put Greece on a parity for stability or neutrality with that state. During my Olympic years, Greece saw the reign of a king, the rule of the colonels, and finally welcome democracy.

Certainly the idea of an Olympic neutral zone might help provide immunity from politics, but then it might not be really neutral. If the site were in Greece, then teams presumably would arrive via Athens, and if Greece happened to have a political upheaval or be at war with another country, would their athletes be allowed in? If you overcome that, by creating a Vatican-style city, would the Olympic country need its own airport, port, and governmental infrastructure? Will the place lie dormant for four years between competitions? You could not expect federations to have their world championships there between the Games.

The more one delved into this subject the more one saw the difficulties, which loomed almost as large as those facing the movement before Moscow. Yet the debate that this created showed that there are people, outside the movement, who are eager to see the Olympic Games sustained as a cornerstone of peace and goodwill. Because of that I am deeply grateful to Karamanlis for pursuing the concept. His country has, of course, permanent links, both ancient and modern, with the Games. Olympia, where Coubertin first thought of the idea of reviving the Games, houses the International Olympic Academy, now a thriving institute, where young people go each year to learn about the Olympic Movement and where trainers and coaches have their seminars. Indeed a permanent site for the Games in Greece was canvassed after the first modern Olympic Games of 1896. It is curious that some governments opposing the holding of the Games in Moscow after the Soviet entry into Afghanistan strongly advocated the Greek idea. President Carter told me he would gladly back such a scheme, adding, "We have a large Greek community," which seems to me an entirely irrelevant reason.

At the time of the European track and field championships in Athens in 1982, Karamanlis again made an appeal for a permanent Olympic site in Greece. I would certainly like to see the centenary of the renovation of the modern Games held there in 1996.

Although I left the IOC in funds, which have now increased considerably, at times I was inclined to sympathise with Avery Brundage who said, as only a rich man could, that money was a nuisance and unimportant. He was always frightened that television rights, the sole source of great income, would not continue forever, especially if the three major American networks could form a consortium to dictate terms, which is currently prevented by antitrust and monopoly laws. This has not happened but, after Los Angeles, direct satellite transmissions, besides closed-circuit arrangements and video cassettes, will alter the situation. There may be pirating of satellite transmissions, which could endanger copyright in the future. As politics must be faced so must the good and bad aspects of money. My aim, assisted by Count de Beaumont, chairman of my Finance Commission, was to create a reserve to ensure against the unforeseen, such as the cancellation of the Games, which has already happened three times, during the world wars.

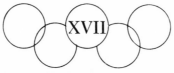

Drugs in Sport

The most obnoxious aspect of sport, and specifically that of international competition, is the abuse of drugs to aid performance. Though it is cheating, this practice is growing and becoming more and more subtle. As the Medical Commission of the IOC and other sporting medical committees catch up with the new methods being used, so scientists work to outwit them with some new invention or discovery. It is like crime and the security business: while the manufacturers endeavour to make safes that cannot be cracked, so the crooks evolve new ways of attacking them. In sport this developed into the creation of the so-called artificial man or woman and the situation is far more serious than is widely believed. Not only does the use of drugs put the individual's welfare at risk, but it also jeopardises the whole future spirit of sport. It is more insidious than even the greatest commercial and political exploitation. Once suspicion is aroused that a competitor, or a group of competitors, is using artificial aid and achieving victories by abnormal margins, then the defeated become dismayed and disillusioned. Unfair practices undermine the whole concept of competition. I have encountered this to a small degree among Olympic competitors, but I see it as the tip of an iceberg leading to the destruction of competition as we know it unless attitudes change and the desire for victory is properly harnessed to the rules of the game.

In some countries there are institutes of sports medicine, where the study of physiology and training techniques can lead to new developments to enhance performance and treat injury, but I suspect strongly that in some of them there are departments that are developing anabolic steroids to create muscle growth, drugs to retard the onset of puberty, and refinements in the stimulant drugs such as amphetamines.

The IOC has led the campaign to stamp out drug taking in sport and it has an immense fight on its hands. There is progress, with more laboratories around the world and a growing call for instant testing. In Norway some competitors were called for tests when they were at an airport about to depart with a team, while in Britain the rowing authorities instituted tests on oarsmen at twenty-four hours' notice during winter training. These are pioneering contributions to tackling this awesome problem, and more must follow to the point where refusal or the avoidance of such testing methods brings about a weight of suspicion and ultimate disqualification.

This sinister end of sports medicine is not, I feel, unrelated to its simple beginning. For many years sports medicine, though it was not called such, meant the sight of a trainer or doctor running on to the field to give first aid. Cold water was the usual reviver, but even that practice has changed, questionably.

The use of pain-killing sprays is now widespread in games like rugby, and I wonder whether such aids are not suppressing injury. After all, pain is merely nature's way of warning; remove it and you are surely taking a risk.

The IOC Medical Commission was first formed in 1961 under the chairmanship of Lord (then Sir Arthur) Porritt. It was brought into being because of a need to determine femininity and, after the death of the Danish cyclist Knud Jensen in trials at the Rome Games the previous year, was extended to control doping, and later the use of anabolic steroids. Although it consists of doctors, I continued the policy of a nonmedical IOC chairman with the appointment of Prince de Mérode of Belgium.

It is chance that ordains people to be of one sex or the other. With the increasing number of women competing in sports previously restricted to men, especially in track and field, it became necessary to ascertain without doubt the sex of competitors. The object was not to distinguish man from woman, but to establish a line dividing femininity and masculinity. There had been suspicions that certain outstanding women athletes were more masculine than feminine, and to avoid the suspicion, pain, and embarrassment that this caused, the commission set up a femininity test. The tests are carried out with the utmost discretion and only in a few instances have they proved positive. One, not at the Olympic Games, was publicised, but the happier outcome was that the woman subsequently married and now has children.

Once a woman has been tested, at the Games or by an international federation's medical committee, and carries the correct identification there is no need for a further test. Thus many of the tests are carried out before a competitor reaches Olympic level and that is an aid to secrecy. The International Amateur Swimming Federation stood out for a long time against tests, asserting that swimsuits clearly disclose the sex of the competitor. We have come a long way since that naïve view, and swimming now takes the Olympic line on the matter.

As sport developed, so did the study of the biological effects on sportsmen of drugs and other aids to high performance. The Eastern Europeans, especially the East Germans, were among the first in the field here, and I recall going to a physical training centre in Zagreb, Yugoslavia, in 1971 where the physiologists and biochemists had worked out the average age at which competitors reach their peak in a particular sport. For instance, if the 1,500-metre run was won most often by someone between the age of 19.9 and 20.3 (I am only guessing at the actual figure), they would note what athletes they had who might reach that particular age in an Olympic year.

Governments have also been studying the risks of drug addiction in sport. As long ago as 1959 the French founded the Association Nationale de l'Éducation Physique, which, in turn, set up a doping commission; and the international sports medicine congresses in Paris and Evian have also devoted themselves to the problem of doping.

Since then, most of the larger sporting nations have had meetings of sports doctors to study the problem and, although the French can perhaps claim to be the originators of a doping commission, the IOC certainly developed and explored this line

of research after the Porritt commission, formed in 1961, passed a resolution at the 1962 session in Mexico forbidding dope.

The Italians promoted the International Federation of Sports Medicine (FIMS), which is recognised by the IOC. In addition to the biologists and physiologists who are constantly experimenting with what can be done with the human body, there are the team doctors. Many of the smaller teams can only take one doctor to the Games. He has to do everything from looking after normal ailments that team members suffer to treating serious injuries and practising physiotherapy. The organising committees have always had a strong medical backup, but once doping control was introduced it became an extremely expensive and highly technical affair. An asset bequeathed by the Olympic Games to Olympic cities is the medical control facilities, as in Munich, Montreal, and Moscow. The medical centre of Montreal was put to use again at the Winter Games in Lake Placid, Montreal being two hours distant. The ideal will be to have available certain approved centres throughout the world. They now exist only in a limited way except in some of the major sporting countries, such as Britain, Canada, Germany, and the USSR, and certain of the Eastern bloc countries where medical research into sport has played such an active part in the development of the athlete.

There is also an Olympic Medical Officers Association, recognised by the IOC, with experienced team doctors. My fear is that there will be a plethora of medical organisations, especially as many sports have their own, but the institution of the IOC International Olympic Medical Officers Association for Research in Sports Medicine was also approved at the Rome session in 1982. This can create conflict and dissipation of effort.

The accusing finger on drug taking, particularly anabolic steroids, has been pointed at the Eastern European countries, and that is justified on the evidence of those found who have had positive tests and who subsequently have been banned, particularly by the IAAF. However, it has caused me dismay that there has really been little vigilance against drug taking in the United States. The Americans do not have any drug-testing sports medicine facilities, and the fact that for the Winter Olympic Games those of Montreal, in another country, had to be used is an indication that the Americans have dragged their feet on this question. Of course, in some American cities what one might term social drugs, such as cannabis, can be obtained easily and used casually, and any restriction on human freedom in the United States is questioned. However, staging the Games in Los Angeles does mean the United States will have to have sports drug-testing facilities for the first time.

In spite of the introduction of the IOC regulations, artificial aid through medicine still continues, and dope testing has resulted in the withdrawal of medals from Olympic athletes as well as the banning of a team doctor from future Olympic Games on the grounds that he was responsible for the act of a competitor.

Certain athletes who use artificial stimulants may well be unaware of the implications of what they are doing. Therefore the real responsibility must lie with the athletes' personal doctors, the team doctors, and often the coaches. It is quite possible that an athlete who is prescribed some specific medication may not realise that it is banned. Here again, it is the athletes who suffer for others' errors.

The introduction of anabolic steroids has given the greatest cause for concern in recent years. Anabolic steroids create artificial muscle and improve the appearance. They are used frequently for horses from an early age to obtain a better price in the sales ring, a practice both misleading for purchasers and dangerous for breeding purposes. With athletes, the drug can do untold and permanent damage to their health. A problem here is not only the cost of detection but the amount of time needed for the highly technical tests.

While there is close cooperation between the international federations, who have their own competitions throughout the four-year period of an Olympiad, and the IOC, the Olympic Movement cannot have ultimate control and this has caused anger and dismay. The IAAF reinstated competitors who were banned after a short period so that they could compete in the Moscow Games. I regret that a man I much admired for his courage and leadership, Adrian Paulen, the IAAF president, took a sympathetic view towards these athletes. The reinstatement of these competitors led to an uproar and bitterness among those athletes who respected the rules and realised the inherent dangers of taking drugs. It caused a division within the administrators of sport, for Arthur Gold, the president of the European Athletic Association, who has stoutly opposed the drug takers, bitterly attacked the IAAF and Paulen for their action. One British athlete, Christine Benning, who would have been chosen for Moscow, declined to go because—and I support her view—she did not wish to compete against people who it was proven had broken the rules.

It was not for me to become involved in the federations' problems, but I believe there must be the closest cooperation among all IFs affected by doping, and that once it is definitely proven that an athlete was doped or had received artificial aids in one way or another, the rules must be fully implemented and supported.

The Olympic ideal is to create the complete person—not an artificial one. Unfortunately, through commercialisation and politicisation, this ideal is being subverted and, through the efforts of certain doctors, the body is being more and more tampered with to its own detriment.

Communications

One of the more extraordinary phenomena in my Olympic years has been the ever-growing compulsion around the world to watch the Games on television, but the literal switch-off for the next four years on Olympic matters. Most people know of the Olympic Games as a sporting event or, more recently, as a cause for political upheaval, without knowing very much of the structure and background of the Olympic Movement. Its mystique and complexity have not been properly unravelled and presented in a form that everyone will understand and want to know more about.

Certainly had the problems of Montreal and Moscow not so occupied my term of office I would, as a former newspaperman and someone much aware of the good and the bad of the communications industry, have liked to have developed further the public relations of the Olympic Movement.

When I first became a member, reports and newspaper stories about the IOC usually went no further than describing it as an autocratic body sprinkled with European royals and ruled over by a slave to amateurism. Brundage did not help matters by having a set series of speeches or pronouncements that he made around the world from time to time. He did hold press conferences during and after the sessions, but those few journalists who remember his conferences recall that they were more frustrating than informative. One states that Brundage would never begin a press conference unless John Farrow of the Associated Press was present. "Where's John?" was a typical remark from Brundage as he shuffled his papers and looked about for the familiar figure. It was not so much due to his friendship with Farrow as the realisation that the Associated Press served most American newspapers and radio and TV stations and was, therefore, Brundage's American voice.

Brundage had his own friends among newspapermen, who were of considerable help to him. But with the press as a whole he was extremely terse, an attitude that contributed very largely to the image of his arrogance and the idea of his apparent refusal to admit that the world was changing.

As a former journalist I had a different approach, since I knew exactly what it was like to be asking questions and failing to get replies, and this knowledge stood me in good stead. At least I was able to have a friendly relationship with representatives of the media, including television, with which I was not previously familiar, and with reporters for radio, which is more like the written word.

The IOC Press Commission, set up at Count de Beaumont's instigation in 1964, was the first commission over which I presided. Our original object was to publicise the IOC and kill its image as a lot of old dodos. We succeeded partially in this but not completely. Eventually the commission evolved into a more important body, taking on representatives of the major news agencies—the Associated Press, Reuters, United Press International, Agence France-Presse, and Tass. Also added were representatives of the IFs and NOCs, independent press representatives, and photographers. Finally, representatives of the press in the host cities were brought in.

Some senior members of the IOC belong to the category of those who look down on the press with some contempt. Many of them have had personal brushes with reporters and others have been unfairly criticised by them. IOC members volunteer to give their time freely and are not paid officials. They are doing their best in the interests of the Olympic Movement and sport in their country. Why should they not be indignant when others, by injudicious statements and in the search for self-promotion, create difficulties between the IOC and the media by leaking decisions before they are announced at the regular press briefings?

Once the IOC has taken a decision, all members are bound to implement and report it within their own area and outside that area if they are invited to speak officially and with the approval of the president of the IOC. In this they are fulfilling the role of an ambassador, who may not personally agree with a policy but must abide by his government's decision. All criticism and disagreement should be expressed within the IOC at sessions.

The International Association of Sports Writers (AIPS) has become an important and useful body, but unfortunately it is still not fully represented in the United States, where, in many ways, there is the greatest need for it because of the problems of press accreditation, especially the accreditation of nonsports journalists. The intention is for precedence to be given to sportswriters, who are actually covering the sports in the Games. There has been an increasing demand for places by political and general reporters, because of developments concerning their field of interest, and also by other journalists such as fashion and gossip writers. At Moscow, for the first time, political journalists came near to outnumbering the sportswriters; thus two different sets of accounts of the Games appeared in the papers in parallel, with many political writers seizing on every small incident they could find for the purposes of propaganda. But ultimately, of course, the peripheral parts of the Olympic Movement should give way to the exploits of the competitor.

The IOC has been lucky in its relations with the media because of the high standing of its members in their own country. Moreover, a large number of IOC members have had practical experience of such matters as television—Mohammed Mzali was formerly director general of the Tunisian Broadcasting Authority; Lance Cross was in charge of radio and television sports programmes in New Zealand; Colonel Mohammed Zerguini was at one time minister for posts and telegraphs in Algeria. There has certainly been in the last thirty years a considerable change in the attitude of the IOC towards the media.

At the early Games that I attended, the press stands were crowded with American newspaper and magazine proprietors and even their families, who took up seats that should have been allocated to sportswriters. We have struggled to give priority to the nonprofessional athlete in the arena, but we have also struggled to give priority to the professional, sporting, nonpolitical journalist in the stands.

The number of newspapermen and -women throughout the world who specialise in writing about the Olympic Movement is very small. I do not refer to the many journalists who cover the actual sports, but to those who understand the inner workings and complexities of the IOC, IFs, NOCs, and organising committees. A hard core has been built up, based largely in the international news agencies. It has been possible through the help of these writers to give off-the-cuff briefings, as is done by most government authorities and those conscious of the importance of public relations. At least some people are now fully briefed and they, in their turn, can assist when uninitiated reporters are sent to meetings. This proved invaluable in the crisis before Moscow. Against this, however, the IOC is quite powerless when the great machinery of a national government propaganda agency comes into play. We have been the victim of such bulldozing, in both the East and the West, when it has suited governments to make use of the Olympic Games for political purposes: witness Mexico, Munich, Montreal, and Moscow.

Radio reporting was treated by the IOC in the same way as the written word until the development of commercial radio stations, especially local ones, which has changed and complicated the situation. All major countries have international radio services in various languages for the dissemination of their views and national propaganda. The Voice of America, the BBC World Service, and the international services of other major national companies are listened to throughout the world and broadcast in many languages. It is unusual for these transmissions to be jammed.

After World War II the American government, through the CIA, helped set up two groups of stations, Radio Liberty and Radio Free Europe, which transmitted chiefly to Eastern Europe. Although they claimed they were only broadcasting basic news that the world was free to listen to or not, and although they were recognised by the Helsinki accords, there is no doubt that these stations are different from the Voice of America or the BBC World Service. The former virtually claim to be ethnic stations broadcasting to Eastern European and other countries in their own language, as opposed to being American or European stations broadcasting in a foreign language.

It appears that Radio Liberty and Radio Free Europe received Olympic accreditation after the war and continued to attend unobtrusively up to the time of the Games in Mexico. Their transmissions emanated chiefly from Spain and West Germany. Some of their broadcasters were American citizens; others were without citizenship or had fled their countries for political reasons. It occurred to me that the Olympic Games were being used in this case to attract listeners in Eastern European countries by providing possibly a better service than that supplied by their own accredited broadcasters. Objectively, the "ethnic" services were taking up space that would otherwise have been allocated to national broadcasting stations. Furthermore, all the competing countries had their own allocation of radio broadcasters, and therefore why should certain American allocations be diverted for these additional broadcasts to Eastern Europe, as they were in Mexico and Montreal?

This matter came to a head at the Winter Games in 1976, when it transpired that the organising committee, unknown to the IOC, had granted permission directly to a large number of these broadcasters to transmit from Innsbruck. Protests were received from Eastern Europe and the IOC withdrew the permission, much to the anger of the United States.

The Soviets and Eastern Europeans objected strongly to these accreditations and I believe that they were indeed a misuse of the intended system of accreditations to the Games. Naturally the IOC was attacked by the press in the United States for applying censorship and being against the free exchange of views. It looked as if this might lead to more trouble in Montreal, which is closer to the United States although farther removed from the stations' transmitters in Europe. In view of the fact that allocations had already been made, the stations agreed that they would in no way combine any form of political broadcast or commentary with their reports from the Olympic Games and that all tapes would be available to the IOC. In fact, in view of the large number of languages being used and the length of time of each broadcast, it would have been quite impossible for the IOC to listen to them all. But, though partly a gesture, the agreement kept the matter from blowing up in Montreal, where there were quite enough problems already.

It is difficult to know what would have happened if the broadcasters of these stations had been refused admission by the Soviet Union in 1980, or had obtained entry through some subterfuge and been subsequently discovered broadcasting from Moscow during the Games. This did not occur, but surely the problem will arise again in 1984. It was a game of power politics that was misunderstood by certain sections of the media in the United States, but the professional members of the IOC Press Commission with whom I spoke were adamant that the IOC stand in the matter was completely correct. This was not a political judgement but one based on sporting and professional grounds, in that the people to whom the broadcasts would have been addressed were already well represented and, moreover, that the object of broadcasts from the Games is not politics. Willi Daume worked extremely hard, tactfully, and diplomatically on this very delicate matter and we were both anxious about the eventual outcome.

The best publicity and public relations the IOC can produce are the briefings by the president or director before, after, and during meetings, and the worst are the private press leaks and conferences that members give. These are frequently an embarrassment to the IOC as well as to its president. It is natural that members of the IOC should wish to brief their own home press, but I have frequently found this has led to misinterpretations, misuse of confidential knowledge, and the transmission of incorrect stories when a reported decision has not actually been reached by the IOC.

The IOC's press relations have improved considerably but they can still get better, as can the standards of the journalists themselves.

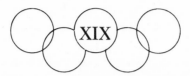

Moscow: An Approach to the Games

On June 4, 1962, we made our way up the gilded staircase of the Kremlin palace overlooking the Moscow River that is used for the official functions held by the Soviet head of state. I followed in protocol order behind Gabriel Gemayel of the well-known Lebanese Maronite family and in front of General Vladimir Stoytchev, who had rallied and led the Bulgarian Army against the Nazis. We were to be introduced to the head of state, President Leonid Brezhnev, by Avery Brundage. We later exchanged polite platitudes with Brezhnev in a baroque room, which had been redecorated in the early thirties for meetings of the party. He was quite stocky, with very black hair and prominent eyebrows. This was the usual reception given by heads of state after the formal opening of IOC sessions. Eighteen years later I was to go to the office of the Council of Ministers on the north side of the Kremlin in order to talk again with this man, then among the most powerful in the world, in a desperate attempt to hold the Olympic Movement together.

The session in Moscow was, in effect, a sort of halfway house. It was ten years since the Soviets had first taken part in the Games at Helsinki and holding a session of the IOC in their capital was an important step towards their bid to stage the Games. There had been a strong presence of the Soviets at Rome in 1960 and the country was already beginning to amaze the world with the way that sport played a very important part in their integrated society. Their mass-participation sports philosophy was similar to the direction Coubertin had hoped the Olympic revival would lead the world.

My first visit to that country produced, as it does for so many visitors, a feeling that was to continue until 1980—a sense of mystery, of not knowing exactly what people were thinking. One admires many facets of Soviet life and is concerned at others. Personally, I find obnoxious any system of government that deprives people of personal freedom, and communism does that. In Soviet society there are still the old roots of the czarist regime and, in fact, the present KGB is based upon the secret service of the Romanov era. After a time one realises that the air of mystery springs most importantly from the continuing presence of an elitist society within the greater society. In my meetings with Soviet officials, there were always people, faces, to whom I was never introduced. At this level, of course, there are always bodyguards, personal assistants, and aides, but in other countries one comes to recognise them. In my visits to the Soviet Union I was constantly asking my staff to find out "Who was that man in the dark suit, with the black eyebrows?" Perhaps it is easy to think there is something sinister about this, but one had the feeling at times that the nameless ones were those pulling the strings.

I have now been to the Soviet Union many times and have met a host of people on the sports administration level. Because the Games were awarded to Moscow when I was president, I developed strong links with several individuals but, unlike almost any other country where there are IOC members, in the Soviet Union I have never been to a private house, never really got to people's roots, to see and understand how they really live and to appreciate that they have the same kind of family problems with which we all have to cope. I do not want to pry into people's lives but I feel it is essential that one know a little about the warts and pockmarks of those with whom one is working so closely. We are all human beings with the same sort of frailties and emotions. Although I have very many friends in the Soviet Union with whom I have laughed, drunk, travelled, and played dominoes, there is still a certain enigma that I do not fully understand.

On the evening of the formal reception in 1962 there was

another held in the Lenin Hills, at which the Soviet Union reminded its guests of a momentous achievement. One of the
guests was Major Yuri Gagarin, the first man to go into space,
whose autographed photograph I still possess. There were
plenty of English-speaking journalists present and I talked with
them to try to brief myself about who was important in the Soviet hierarchy, who was a member of the Politburo, and so on.

Various people whose names meant nothing to me were
pointed out and then I said, "What about the president of the
Soviet Union, Mr. Brezhnev?" who had received me earlier that
day. "Oh, he's just the titular president. He was kicked upstairs—quite unimportant." (Nikita Khrushchev then dominated Soviet politics.) In fact, Brezhnev was subsequently
elected first secretary of the Communist party, giving him the
real power, and later was reelected president in succession to
Nikolai Podgorny. So much for on-the-spot knowledge!

I have no reason to believe that we were followed or
watched for security or espionage reasons in 1962. I would go
out on my own when I felt like it to see the sights and even visited the little Roman Catholic church that lies very close to the
Lubyanka and the Bolshoi Theatre. All the metro signs and
names are in Cyrillic script and I had to count the stations and
compare the script against the metro map to find my way. Oc-
casionally I overshot the station and had to walk back to the
hotel. In fact, once you have thrown your few kopecks into the
automatic gates you can spend the whole day travelling to any
station without paying another fare. The lines were extended
specially for the Olympic Games, but the metro stations themselves have not altered. They are vast, ornate, palatial, and im-
maculately clean compared to the tube stations of London, New
York, or Paris. I think that the greatest joy of the Moscow
metro, when I last travelled on it, was the lack of graffiti, post-
ers, and advertising.

My good friend General Stoytchev had hunted with the
Quorn foxhounds when military attaché in London and had
been used to buying his bowler hats at Lock's, the famous London hatters. He was elected at the 1952 Helsinki session and,
though junior to me in IOC protocol ranking, was much my senior in years. As he was a hero of the Soviet Union we could go

anywhere we wished and he took me to see the equestrian schools, which are controlled by the military, as well as to the racecourse. The Moscow racecourse is antiquated and the stands look prerevolutionary, although they are in fact of a later date. On one visit to Moscow with my wife I was anxious to see the racing but was informed there was none that day. The female interpreter who was allocated to us was somewhat puritanical and did not think racing a suitable sport, especially as the jockeys, whether riding or driving trotters, are professionals. We went up to the racecourse and I said there must be a meeting that night because of the long queue. "I will make enquiries," said the girl. She did so, and then explained that the queue was waiting to buy racecards but there was no racing until the next day. Through her, I asked some of the people in the queue why they were so anxious to obtain racecards a day early. "So we can choose which of our horses to back," came the reply. As all the horses belonged to the state, the Russians were betting on what they considered "their" horses.

From the 1962 session onwards the Soviet NOC began working very hard to be awarded the Games for Moscow. I believe the Russians were acting in the best sporting tradition and wished to contribute to the Olympic family, of which they felt they were now part. Any city that hosts the Games is naturally anxious to show itself and its community at its best.

Their first application to stage the Games, at Amsterdam in 1970, having failed, the Russians made their second bid in Vienna in 1974. This was the first time the Games were awarded under my presidency and Moscow had only one rival, Los Angeles. I ruled that the decision be announced as unanimous and the voting figures were never issued. In truth, the vote in favour of Moscow was almost unanimous.

In 1974 most of the West voted for Moscow. Had it become a political vote the IOC, which is basically conservative, might have voted differently. But this was the height of East-West detente and, in any case, the voting was based purely on sporting grounds. The result was almost universally welcomed. Some doubts were expressed as to the ability of the Soviets, for all their bureaucratic resources, to administer the Games. But no question was asked about their sporting and technical ability, which was indisputable.

Suggestions have been made that President Richard Nixon had made a deal that Los Angeles would not make a strong bid to allow the Games to go to Moscow. However, this would have been quite unacceptable to the USOC, the Los Angeles delegation, and, of course, the IOC.

Many felt that the Soviet Union was opening its doors to all for the first time and the critical visitors might assist. This was confirmed by Richard Owen in *The Times* of London on July 21, 1982: "The Muscovites have good reason to be grateful to the tourists. . . . Almost all the improvements in the antiquated procedures you encounter in shops, hotels and restaurants stem from the influx of foreigners into Moscow two years ago for the Olympic Games." On the other hand, there were some early and consistent political critics of giving the Games to any Communist state, and when the Soviets entered Afghanistan, many more people jumped on the bandwagon.

It might seem strange that a basically conservative organisation like the IOC could swing so heavily to support a Communist city. Few among us were naïve enough not to realise that in putting on the Games Moscow would present the Soviet way of life, which meant propounding communism. But every city that has staged the Games has wanted to mirror the country and lifestyle that surround it. After all, Soviet television viewers have had to watch a lot of capitalist Olympic Games. No doubt people thought in casting their vote for Moscow they were supporting the mood of detente. That apart, on the question of sporting infrastructure and organisation, there was only one candidate. The Russians brought a professionalism to the way they absorbed the rules and regulations of international sport and saw to it that they were understood.

In my dealings with the Soviets, whether official or sporting, I have found that it takes some time to come to an agreement, whether over a television contract or a point of protocol, but that once their word has been given it stands. I made several visits to the Soviet Union to see the highest authorities there. The first of these visits was in August 1973, when I saw Premier Kosygin in the Kremlin for the first time. He reiterated the guarantee that the organising committee had been able to report back to the IOC before, namely that all NOCs recognised by the IOC would be admitted, whether the Soviet Union had diplomatic relations with the governments of their countries or not. I met Kosygin at a roundtable conference with Soviet IOC member Andrianov and Sergei Pavlov, then president of the USSR NOC, who was also the equivalent of minister for sport. My qualms at that time were that the Soviets would concoct some device to keep Israel, specifically, and other countries with whom they did not have diplomatic relations, out of the Games. As it turned out there was little need to worry about that.

After we had discussed the Olympic problems through Kosygin's interpreter, the premier said he knew my country. Since I have an English accent and a title it is assumed sometimes that I am British. I was about to explain I was Irish when he said, in English I think, "Not Dublin, but Belfast." It turned out that when as minister for light industry he had been in London, he was sent to Belfast to visit a factory. I later met a British civil servant at the Soviet desk in Downing Street at a dinner party given by the Garrick Club and he told me he had accompanied Kosygin on this trip. I gather the visit to the factory was brief and left them with a certain amount of time to spare. As a result Kosygin probably learned more about some of the back streets of Belfast than most Englishmen who are responsible for the affairs of the North of Ireland ever do.

On November 19, 1976, I was to return to Moscow to see President Podgorny. This time I was accompanied by Ignati Novikov of the organising committee (a vice-president of the Presidium), Vitaly Smirnov, who served on the Executive Board and was a vice-president of the IOC, and Sergei Pavlov. It was very much the same routine as before and again I was given an assurance about the admission of all recognised NOCs. Podgorny left office shortly afterwards, to be replaced by Brezhnev.

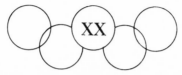

Moscow: The Afghanistan Problem

$\mathbf{M}$y initial reaction to the Christmas-time news of the Soviet incursion into Afghanistan in 1979 was not one of alarm. Absorbed as I was at that time with my children and grandchildren, I certainly did not envisage the crisis developing in the manner it did. I suppose it comes from a diplomatic writing background, but I am cautious when I see the word "invasion." It is the sort of word used about the other side.

Yet the Soviets were in Afghanistan in force, saying that they had been invited in to put down rebels. There were, however, other more subtle political interpretations, such as that they wanted to strengthen their southern flank because of events in Iran and the oil in the Persian Gulf. The U.S. Embassy in Moscow did not take long to formulate its advice to Washington. Grain embargoes, action over industrial contracts, and broken trade agreements would hurt Americans, but the Moscow Olympic Games were vulnerable to attack.

In the first two weeks of January 1980 the boycott campaign began to roll. At the outset it sounded like a threat and many of the statements from the White House indicated to me that Washington was not conversant with the Olympic structure. The glib ideas about moving the Games were neither politic nor desirable, and the idea of postponing events for a year took no account of the complexity of the international sporting programme or the strict IOC rule that the Games take place in the last year of the Olympiad.

The first positive sign of trouble reached me on January 28. I was in Ireland for a company board meeting when a transatlantic telephone call reached me from John Moore, a former American ambassador to Ireland, whom I knew well. He asked me whether I would see a Mr. Lloyd Cutler, counsel to the president of the United States. He inferred that it was about the Olympic Games and Afghanistan. I had, after all the rumblings coming from Washington and Whitehall, expected that some sort of approach would be made, at least for information. I was, as it turned out, to get a great shock. The meeting was arranged for February 2 at my Dublin house. It was the day of an international rugby match which meant that cars would be parked across my drive, if not actually in it, as the ground is only three hundred yards away. Cutler, though, did not want the world to know he was visiting me, so we kept things quiet. After lunch Moore and Cutler arrived in a Bank of Ireland car (Moore was a director), passing through the crowd going to the rugby match unnoticed, and proceeded to my library. Cutler is a tall, pleasant, well-mannered man whose head seemed to drop at times, giving you the feeling he was looking at you out of the top of his eyes with the stabbing penetration of a lawyer, which he was.

I discovered that Cutler had not flown in from Washington to discuss, but rather to instruct. It was not a question of examining the problem from all its aspects. There was only one position, the political one, as far as he was concerned.

Cutler gave a long speech explaining politically and geographically the dangers of the Soviet "invasion," with the possibilities of their pushing down to the Persian Gulf to cut off the oil supplies to the Western world. On determining that this might be the Soviet strategy, he had come with a demand from the president of the United States that the International Olympic Committee either postpone or cancel the Games. I was rather angry. Here again was the American attitude of bringing out the bulldozer to save someone from an awful fate, or what America thought was an awful fate. It was this sense of arrogance, not personally shown by Cutler but evident in the highhanded approach of the White House, that raised my hackles.

I told him and Moore that whatever were my personal views about what the Soviet Union had done or not done in

Afghanistan, I had a job to do as president of the IOC and could not allow my political views to interfere with the undertaking that we had given to Moscow and the athletes of the world; the second point was important and I stressed it. It was not a question of where the Games were being staged, but that they were being staged. Once that had been decided a vast number of international and national organisations and thousands and thousands of individuals were legally and morally committed.

Cutler told me to my surprise that under Olympic rules the Games could only be held with an international truce in effect and this rule should be invoked. It turned out the information had come from a history of the ancient Games, held when there was a truce among the Hellenic states. These Games had inspired Coubertin, but he had not been able to follow their dictates, even to the exclusion of women.

Our conversation showed too that Cutler did not realise IOC members were not their country's representatives to the committee, nor did he understand the rules of the international federations and their independence, and neither, I suspect, did he understand the position of the national Olympic committees. As the meeting went on I became more and more concerned about the ignorance of Olympic matters at the White House.

On the question of war interfering with the Olympic Games, I told Cutler that the modern Games had three times been cancelled during the two great wars, when travel was impossible. The Olympic Movement then being very much a European stronghold, it was not possible to celebrate the Games due in 1916. Tokyo, which was due to stage the Games of 1940, withdrew the invitation well before that because of the Sino-Japanese conflict. That decision may have been inspired by the IOC, but the initiative came from the hosts. In 1940, the Games scheduled for Helsinki had to be cancelled, as were those for London in 1944. Although the truce was not in the rules, the IOC could call for one, as we did when the United States was fighting in Vietnam and Korea. Those wars continued, but so did the Games.

I maintained a calm in the face of all this ignorance, which was all the sadder coming from a man of such intelligence, but I think the president's representative saw my wrath when he de-

livered the White House message. He told me that the USOC
was to request a full session of the IOC on the instructions of the
president of the United States to cancel or postpone the Games.
I was angered at this request. For years we have been accused
of hypocrisy, of permitting totalitarian states of the right and
left to interfere with the workings of their NOCs, which is
against our rules, and here we had the world's most powerful
democracy crushing that treasured independence in one simple
statement. Whatever the rights and wrongs of the Afghanistan
affair, the judgement of one man, already scrambling for his political life in the American presidential election campaign,
which occurs in the Olympic year, had turned the Olympic
arena into what was to be its own battleground.

I replied to the president's request that under the Olympic
Charter the Games could under no circumstances be postponed
to another year, and to cancel them at this late stage would
have meant a breach of contract for which there were no
grounds within the framework of the agreement.

Cutler then went off to the U.S. Embassy. I bade him farewell from the steps of the house and as I did so I thought, sel-
fishly I suppose, "Oh, God, after Montreal do I deserve this?" As
the car moved off, there was a roar from the rugby stadium a
few hundred yards away. It was that sort of roar that indicates a
try has been scored and it was just the stimulus I needed at that
moment—someone had triumphed on the sporting field and the
delight and satisfaction it gave me at that moment reminded me
of the expectations around the world, as far as the Olympic
Games were concerned.

My first action was to inform the director of the IOC,
Mme. Berlioux, of the outcome of my meeting and get her to
ensure that the president of the USOC, Robert Kane, and Don
Miller, the director, would be available when I arrived in Lake
Placid for the Winter Games in a few days' time. I phoned sev-
eral of my members from Dublin to confirm what they had sus-
pected from the media over the previous two weeks, that the
IOC had another battle on its hands.

I met Kane and Miller on my arrival at the rambling Lake
Placid Country Club on February 7. They told me that on hearing the president's request, relayed to them by Cutler, they had

protested against the interference by the federal government in the affairs of the USOC. They said that under Olympic rules their committee must be autonomous and resist political pressure. That was exactly what I wanted to hear.

Unhappily, the USOC was not as independent as it had been in the past because of the Amateur Athletic Act of 1978 passed by the U.S. Congress, making the USOC virtually the official governing body of all sports in the United States. The constitution of this committee is a complex one in that through the act it is answerable in some ways to the government. It is perhaps ironic that the initiative for this act came largely through the dissatisfaction of Olympic athletes at the way sport was administered and organised in their country as compared with others, and particularly those of Eastern Europe. American disorganisation at Munich led to two important sprinters missing their events because the management failed to understand the twenty-four-hour clock and the difference between 1500 hours and five o'clock. This type of incident led to a campaign to improve sports administration—resulting in the act.

It was designed, and in the most part worked, towards assisting amateur sport in the United States, which had been chaotic due to the rivalry between the football-rich National Collegiate Athletic Association and the conservative but gentlemanly Amateur Athletic Union. Until recently many sports were federated through a division of the AAU rather than direct as in most NOCs. But soon after the act's passage the relationship between government and the USOC was being used by the politicians as an international weapon.

Kane and Miller made it quite clear to me that they had to appear, as instructed by their government, in front of the IOC session to present the government's view. I did not need to, of course, but just for the record I pointed out that no agency, organisation, person, or government instructs anyone to appear before the IOC. That is the prerogative of the IOC and we do not instruct, we invite. There is no compulsion on anyone to compete in the Olympic Games. They are there for those who subscribe to the rules and achieve the necessary standards. The IOC acts in the same manner with officials and organisations. I think that the dignity and decorum that this involves is so much better in creating and preserving sporting friendships and goodwill. I had already planned to ask Kane and Miller to attend an Executive Board meeting to explain their position and it seemed highly probable that they would repeat that before the session, but definitely not at the instruction of a government or its head.

I saw Cutler again on the same day. He had come in from Washington with aides, who were to stay at Lake Placid during the session to lobby against the Moscow Games. Cutler confirmed what Kane and Miller had told me and also informed me that the IOC session, opened normally by the head of state, but by his nominee at the time of the Games, would be opened by Cyrus Vance, secretary of state, rather than by New York Governor Hugh Carey, who had been most helpful at all times and who I had anticipated would be nominated. The function is usually purely ceremonial and I made this point since, with so much ignorance, I did not want Vance to suffer the embarrassment of making a political speech in the wrong place at the wrong time.

I could not be sure how my members would react to the enormity of the situation. I had to consider that the majority of them had right-wing views, with some of them very strong, but after all these were the men who had chosen Moscow for the Games. The Executive Board heard Kane and Miller, and the members shared my view about the United States government's intrusion. Meanwhile there was concern within the IOC secretariat because Vance's speech had not arrived and they could not obtain a copy of it. The normal procedure was for these speeches to be produced well in advance so there was no tedious repetition, and to allow time for translations to be made in French and/or English. People tended to doze off on these ceremonial occasions and I did not want to encourage them. Vance's speech was not available, we were told, and that heightened my suspicion that we were in for a political diatribe.

One or two members were concerned, what with the public attitude of Carter towards the Soviet Union, as they did not want a political demonstration in the session and some of the members of the board, including Beaumont, felt that the formal opening of the session should not take place unless Vance's speech was available in advance for the board to study.

We continued to try to obtain it on the day of the ceremony but Washington was not forthcoming. Then a couple of hours before the event one of my journalist friends came up to my suite with a copy of agency stories giving extracts from the speech, which had been released in Washington to the media for distribution. In other words, it was on the desks of the news editors around the world, but not on the desk of the president of the IOC.

The extracts from the agency message, obviously the most controversial parts, were outrageously political. Vance was virtually ordering the IOC to cancel or postpone the Moscow Games and I realised that parts of the speech could be interpreted as a direct attack on the Soviet Union. In the audience would be Ignati Novikov, who was not only president of the Moscow organising committee but a high Soviet government official. Having reread certain passages, I could envisage that Novikov and his entourage would almost certainly walk out. They were, after all, in Lake Placid at the invitation of the IOC to present a progress report on the preparations for the Moscow Games. They were, in effect, joint guests of the IOC, the Lake Placid organising committee, and the USOC, and were in the country whose government was trying to torpedo the Games they were going to stage. In those circumstances some of Vance's words were bound to offend the IOC.

I was in a predicament, for while it seemed fairly certain that the Vance speech had been cleared by the White House and there was very little chance of a change of course, I knew, as an old newspaperman, that an advance speech could be killed or amended until delivery. I had to act cautiously so I called in my senior vice-president, Vitaly Smirnov. I warned him of what might happen and asked that whatever was said he and Constantin Andrianov, his Soviet colleague, should remain throughout the ceremony.

About half an hour before the ceremony was due to begin Vance arrived with Cutler and some of his assistants in my hotel suite. They walked in unannounced. My wife and IOC Vice-President Kiyokawa were with me. Vance walked in smiling, as though there were nothing wrong in the world. I immediately demanded to know why I had not received a copy of his speech although it had been issued to the media, and impressed upon him that from the extracts I had read the speech was outrageously political. He retorted, "That is what I believe and that is what I am going to say." He then passed over the entire text, which I read through. Obviously the press had lifted the most controversial extracts but it still remained, to my mind, inappropriate to say the least.

I reread the speech, having left the room, while Kiyokawa chatted with Vance and the others, and I called Smirnov into my bedroom and told him that I did not think it was appropriate for Novikov or the organising committee to attend the opening ceremony of the session. As an entity I now felt the speech was even worse than the extracts indicated. If the American government was going to abuse the occasion and use it for political ends, I did not want anyone involved in the Olympic Movement to respond with a counterdemonstration. Smirnov took back the message and twenty minutes before the opening ceremony the chairs for the Moscow delegation were quietly removed; but the incident was not unnoticed or unrecorded because a photographer spotted what was happening.

In his speech Vance reminded the audience that the ancient Olympics had symbolised some of humanity's noblest principles. Foremost among these was peace. With this no one disagreed, nor with his view that the doves being released during the opening ceremonies of the Games symbolised peace. He then continued to emphasise that when the Games were held in Elis they marked "a truce of the gods." During this truce, open warfare against or by the host city was forbidden. Perhaps it was forgotten that in 1970, at the time of the award of the Winter Games for 1976 to Denver, the United States was in Southeast Asia, but this was never raised as an issue. He continued by stating: "We already see the nation selected as a host of the summer games describing its selection as 'recognition of the correctness of its foreign policy course' and 'the enormous advances in the struggle for peace.' "

Vance was quoting from a *Handbook for Party Activists*, published in Moscow in 1979 before the Afghanistan affair. This touched a raw nerve, but it was an error (in IOC terms) on the part of the Soviet Union that was blown up out of all proportion. Some Russians might have thought that having the Games in Moscow was a recognition of something or other; all it did was recognise the Soviet Union's place in the Olympic Movement and its competence to organise the Games, nothing more, and I made this point firmly when I later met Brezhnev.

Then Vance stated: "Responsibility for the matter should not be shifted to the athletes. This would only force them to carry a burden which properly belongs to the leaders of the Olympic Movement. None of us wants our athletes to suffer but neither should we let them be exploited."

The reaction to this was that the United States, together with some of its allies, was itself exploiting athletes for political reasons, and that the Games were the Games of the IOC being held in Moscow and therefore had no connection with the politics of the country in which the Games were to take place. The secretary of state, as President Carter had done already and did subsequently, said he supported the Olympic Movement and its principles but did not want to see the Olympic Movement damaged. There could be no doubt that the steps now being taken by the White House were, in fact, causing great damage, and had they been successful the Olympic Movement might have been wrecked—on the altar of American political expediency.

Vance went on: "The preferable course would be to transfer the Games from Moscow to another site, or multiple sites, this summer. Clearly there are practical difficulties but they could be overcome. There is also a precedent for canceling the Games. Or it would be possible, with a simple change of rules, to postpone the Games for a year or more."

I had the feeling as these words came down from the rostrum that there were a lot of white knuckles gripping the arms of chairs to conceal anger. It was the depth of insensitivity before an audience whose lives had encompassed the propagation of the Olympic Movement for many years. It indicated to me that this was not just about Afghanistan; it was the campaign of a president trying to squirm his way out of an electoral defeat already firmly written ten months before the election by the American voters.

Vance did not appear to see that there was a firm commitment with the Moscow organising committee, as there was with Lake Placid, whose Winter Games were about to open, as well as with Los Angeles in 1984. "A simple change of rules" is not as simple as might be thought, as it would tend to split the Olympic Movement and international sports throughout the world. Then came Vance's final political statement: "Let me make my government's position clear—we will oppose the participation of an American team in the Olympic Games in the capital of an invading nation. This position is firm. It reflects the deep conviction of the United States Congress and American people."

However, a partial restriction on grain sales, subsequently lifted with the Soviet Union still in Afghanistan, was the sum total of American economic action. While that part of the world which regarded the Soviet action as an invasion deplored it over the months to follow, the credibility of the American government was stretched.

The White House speechwriters had been so busy thinking of politics that they forgot to include the words for Vance to open the session. It is the only session I have attended where speeches have been made and the session never officially opened. This was unique to what was probably the most important session ever held since the foundation of the IOC in 1894.

Vance's speech was greeted in absolute silence by everybody. It was a demonstration at an Olympic event of which I approved and the world took note of it. Some of my members were so incensed they did not attend the reception given later by Vance; I certainly did not expect the Soviets to appear nor did they, but I thought there might be some value in talking to Vance, though few shared that view. I may have thanked him for a drink and left.

When Cutler had left my house just a week before, I knew that the lines were drawn for the biggest battle in Olympic history. Vance's speech had drawn the IOC membership together as though someone had lassoed them with an enormous rope. On every side, in the corridors of the country club, in the restaurant, and among callers to my suite, there were words of disgust at what the United States government was doing and the way it was going about it.

What I needed to do was to turn this unity into an expression of feeling that was unanimous. I realised that the idea of a terse resolution of condemnation of the United States and support for Moscow could easily be misinterpreted and might be difficult for all my members to support. So I drew a few friends round me, including James Worrall, the Canadian member who had been such a help to me in Montreal's troubles, and we devised a shrewd tactic to counter the boycott. After much lobbying and rewriting, the president of the IOC's statement was produced and the entire membership supported it.

When the full session of the IOC had its first meeting, Kane and Miller made their appearance and it seemed that Kane was putting forward his government's case without any heart. The figures from the government about the percentage of the population against the Games in Moscow and other related questions seemed to me to be an unfairly weighted opinion-poll exercise. Kane, in questioning by the members, said that prior to Carter's request the USOC had made a firm statement against a boycott.

"Oh dear, I've got myself in an awful tangle."

DAILY MAIL — MARCH 17, 1980.

History will tell its own story, but I am convinced that the credibility of the IOC was not lost when it abided by its word in holding the Games for those athletes who wished to attend. It has never been the object of the IOC to compel anyone to take part in the Games anywhere; it is up to each individual's conscience.

Meanwhile, in Mexico City the Association of National Olympic Committees held a meeting and declared their support for the IOC. Carter, redoubling his attack, not only sent a demand to Lake Placid that we move or cancel the Games but told the Soviet Union that unless their troops were out of Afghanistan by February 20, he would do all he could to stop countries from competing.

Prime Minister Thatcher, of course, was echoing almost every word Carter uttered on the subject, while there was a worrying situation in Australia, where then Prime Minister Fraser was also acting in a belligerent manner. The Australian NOC received a letter from the prime minister stating the view of the government, which supported Carter, but the NOC's executive board considered it and without taking any position on the matter passed the letter to the IOC. On looking back now it makes me feel cynical that the British government later ignored the United States' requests for anti-Soviet action when it meant an economic sacrifice in relation to the Soviet gas pipeline to Germany, with detente further away and the Soviets still in Afghanistan; while Fraser fretted about losing the Commonwealth Games in Brisbane.

The debate in the IOC session continued over two days and I reiterated my view that Vance's speech had made the members think how much the American reaction was interference for political ends. There were members, however, who held reservations about the course the debate was taking, members from Chile and Malaysia whose governments were obviously not sympathetic to Olympic Games in Moscow after Afghanistan.

Towards the end of the discussion I called on Reginald Alexander, a fine writer in English, Willi Daume, for diplomatic reasons, and James Worrall to help shape the statement. I then rewrote sections of it and there was some tidying up done in the session, but the final statement was approved. The crux of it was that all seventy-three members present at the session were unanimous that the Games must be held in Moscow as planned. It was a document put down to my name, but with everyone's support.

The statement reminded all that, first, the Games had been awarded to the city of Moscow and an agreement signed among all parties on October 23, 1974. All preparations had been made in keeping with the terms of that agreement and consistently with the rules of the IOC. Second, the prime responsibility of the IOC is to the young athletes of the world and to ensure that the Olympic Games are held every four years in accordance with the principles and rules of the IOC. Third, the International Olympic Committee was fully aware and sensitive to the world conditions that had created the most serious challenge to confront the Olympic Games. Fourth, many governments had stated that the athletes of their countries would not be encouraged, or might even be forbidden, to take part in the 1980 Games in Moscow, and the USOC had made representations to the IOC at the request of the president of the United States. These had been debated and discussed as had all other suggestions. Fifth, all 142 recognised national Olympic committees are bound by the Olympic rules. It is they alone that can accept or refuse invitations to the Olympic Games after consultations with their members, the majority of whom represent federations with a sport on the Olympic programme. The international federations have the responsibility for the technical aspects of the Games and these federations had always supported the IOC.

My statement noted that many NOCs had been placed in a very difficult position in relation to their government and public opinion. Every effort would be made by the IOC, its members, and the NOCs to inform the governments and public of the principles and aims of the Olympic Movement. I recalled that the final date for acceptance or refusal of the invitation to compete in the Games was May 24, 1980. It was carefully worded: "The IOC recognises particularly the difficulties with the United States Olympic Committee and encourages it to continue its efforts to make possible the participation of its athletes in the Games. Also the IOC urges the Organising Committee in Moscow and the National Olympic Committees of the USSR to inform the highest authorities in their government of the circumstances which have created these difficulties for so many NOCs."

My statement then stressed that it was the very existence of the Olympic Games, the Olympic Movement, and the organisation of sport through the international federations that were at stake. Finally, my statement said the IOC could not solve the political problems of the world but called upon governments of all countries, and in particular those of major powers, to come together to resolve their differences, while "I, as President of the IOC, and all members will do everything in our power to assist in this so that the Games of the XXII Olympiad can take place in the right atmosphere."

We then turned away from this problem to face the more immediate one of the Lake Placid Games. They were clearly close to bankruptcy; furthermore, there was not enough transport, and from the word "go" it did not seem to work properly.

I still did not know who was going to open the Lake Placid Games, as President Carter was ensconced in the White House with an election ahead and the problem of the American hostages in Tehran, which I believe was the uppermost concern in United States public opinion, besides having entered the Olympic arena. Then Carter stated that neither at Los Angeles in 1932 nor at the previous Winter Games in the United States had the president opened the Games. At the last moment I was informed that he had delegated his authority to Vice-President Walter Mondale.

I was not allowed to take my wife to the opening ceremony in my car. She had to travel in a bus, which arrived late with many other IOC members after the ceremony was underway. I wish I had been there a little earlier myself to hear Governor Carey making what I understand was an election speech before the ceremony began.

As we were walking out from the ceremony, Mondale broke ranks to shake hands with what I presume were constituents, as they were all saying, "I'm from such-and-such a place in Minnesota." We could have been at an after-mass political meeting for a general election in Ireland. Mondale did not give the usual formal reception after the opening but returned immediately to Washington. Carey also left after we had been photographed together with Senator Moynihan—an Irish group.

I believe to this day that if the Afghanistan Olympic question had been dealt with diplomatically, as opposed to politically, by Carter, it is quite possible that talks might have been held with the Soviets to point out the dangers of the boycott of the Games. In the end everybody to whom I spoke said we would have to go to Moscow, even if there were very few NOCs participating.

In the ice hockey at Lake Placid, the United States beat the Soviet Union and won the gold medal. This led to a great show of chauvinism by the United States, and Carter immediately contacted the coach and invited the team to an official reception at the White House. I am told he did not do this short-circuiting through the USOC and indeed, although this was rectified later, even forgot to invite Eric Heiden, who had won five gold medals—apart from the rest of the United States team, who had competed in a very fair and sporting manner. This move by Carter again antagonised the USOC and most of the athletes. It added to the politicisation, for I believe it was not a reception for the team because they had won a gold medal, but because they had beaten the Soviet Union in gaining it.

In spite of the difficulties with transportation there was some excellent and well-organised sport at the Lake Placid Games. When the flame was extinguished, I took the opportunity to add a few words to those that are normally used to close the Games. I told the world:

> The spectators of these Games have contributed to the understanding which we in the Olympic Movement believe in; an understanding which is without race, religion or colour. I would like to thank the media . . . and all those who contributed to the success of the Games. Ladies and gentlemen, I feel these Games have proved that we do something to contribute to the mutual understanding of the world, what we have in common and not what our differences are. If we can all come together it will be for a better world and we shall avoid the holocaust which may well be upon us if we are not careful.

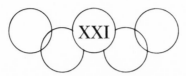

Moscow: The Final Journey

The journey from Lake Placid to Moscow was going to be a tortuous one, I knew, but I certainly did not think that the world's greatest democracy would bring into play such power and force to prevent an international organisation from pursuing what it believed to be the proper course. On hearing of the IOC decision in Lake Placid, Carter lost little time, after the February 20 deadline, in announcing that the United States would not send a team to the Games. That was a clear case of political interference and, unless the USOC rebuffed it, we could move towards taking action against the committee, and that in turn would affect the Los Angeles Games in 1984. That, though, was a trail I did not want to follow.

I resolved at Lake Placid to avoid that sort of manoeuvring. As far as I was concerned the IOC had made its position clear. I was now ready to go anywhere I was invited to talk about the problems and, if required, to help, but I was not going on a propaganda tour of the world's NOCs imitating Cutler or the other American emissaries. I was criticised by some people in the months between the Winter Games and Moscow for "staying in my Dublin castle," but I could see no value in going around the world making statements that might be misused and misinterpreted, only to draw politicians' counterstatements, which would suffer the same fate.

On reflection, I do not think anyone realised that the debate would range so widely, cause such deep divisions between old friends, or reach the point of a prime minister of Australia acting as a spokesman for President Carter; of the USOC debating national security; of the British Parliament voting on British participation in Moscow; of the West German NOC holding its debate live on television. My voice raised too loudly amid all that would probably have done more damage than good. I spent many hours of the day and night on the telephone, obtaining information and passing it on. I tried to be the catalyst that could help others to make their decision. After Lake Placid, the ball was in the court of the NOCs, the IFs, and the national sports associations. Those who wanted advice sought it, and certainly found it with me and my colleagues on the IOC.

There were a myriad of decisions I had to consider. Doubtless history will show I made mistakes. Some of the problems were extremely difficult, for example, if and when to see Brezhnev and Carter. In Lake Placid, Berthold Beitz was among those who urged me to go to the White House and then to Moscow. However, I felt that Carter, having set his position without consultation, had been rebuffed by the IOC statement and would not have been very receptive. I also cancelled a long-planned trip to Moscow in March for a meeting of the IOC Press Commission because I believed the Soviets might make public relations capital out of it.

Having set course for a boycott, Carter then tried to organise alternative Games, which were doomed to failure from the outset. He and his supporters though went through the motions, more I feel in a deception of the public than anything else. The British government lent their weight and were part of a Gilbert and Sullivan style meeting in Geneva to discuss the arrangements. What they did not understand was that without the cooperation of the international federations no such competition would be possible. The IFs agree, for their own benefit as much as for that of the Olympic Movement, not to hold major competitions just before or during the period of the Games. None would have sanctioned alternative meetings and thus national federations would not be able to compete.

In tandem with that was pressure on IOC members and the IFs from American embassies to move the Games from Moscow or postpone them. But of course their biggest campaign was the internal one, rousing public opinion against the Soviets, which is never very difficult in the United States. Pressure was brought to bear on the competitors, many of whom bitterly resented Carter's actions. Several, including Anita DeFrantz, an American oarswoman, acted bravely in putting the Olympic case to legal test, which unhappily was to be submerged.

In my telephone calls to the United States and particularly to Don Miller, I detected that all this pressure was causing a weakness of resolve. Miller called me on one occasion to talk about postponement, which he knew very well was impossible. I felt that he was under some sort of obligation to raise the matter. At about the same time I had another transatlantic call from Cutler and much of the conversation took a similar line.

In Britain the debate raged. Lord Carrington, the foreign minister, met the heads of sport to dissuade them from going to Moscow. The British Olympic Association (BOA) had several meetings and arranged its crucial one a few days after the question was debated in the House of Commons on March 17. This was not a matter for Parliament, and when one reads the record of the proceedings, the standard of debate and the messiness of argument and misinformation did that chamber no good.

There were also debates in the House of Lords. Although entitled to take part in the debate I did not as, first of all, I was the neutral president of the IOC and, secondly, I have always been careful, as an Irishman, not to be involved in British domestic situations. Sir Denis Follows came under the most bitter attacks but spoke with the voice of the British Olympic Association. He was ably supported in the House of Commons by Denis Howell, the former minister with responsibility for sport in the Labour government, who was naturally concerned at the contempt with which certain politicians were using the athletes to accomplish political objectives that they would not undertake themselves through the normal parliamentary and diplomatic channels. The former British prime minister Edward Heath also spoke against the boycott.

While there was a large majority in favour of not sending a team, a large number of MPs abstained, and I was never quite sure whether this was because of indecision or repugnance to a "Have you stopped beating your wife?" type of question. The debate went on with competitors in their tracksuits sitting in the public gallery. In spite of the Mother of Parliaments pronouncing thus, the BOA voted a few days later to go. The country was then divided, but the decision undoubtedly helped keep the greater part of Western Europe in the Games.

Meanwhile, the USOC met at Colorado Springs, Colorado, its headquarters, to discuss national security, which to my way of thinking is not a matter for an NOC—an organising committee, yes. It was, of course, a significant enough gathering to be addressed by Vice-President Mondale. Most NOCs would have refused to be addressed by politicians, other than a minister for sport if he was funding the NOC. Mondale was detailed to speak by Carter, who was honorary president of the USOC and claimed right of voice. Many years ago, when the late Eamon De Valera ceased to be prime minister of Ireland and became president and head of state, he retired from being patron of the Olympic Council of Ireland, and ever since then my own NOC has not had political officers or patrons.

The emotional attitude of the Colorado Springs meeting is summed up in part of Mondale's remarks: "If we and our allies and friends fail to use every single peaceful means available to preserve peace, what hope is there that peace will long be preserved? The President, the Congress and the American people understand that a world which travels to the Moscow Games devalues its condemnation [of the invasion of Afghanistan] and offers its complicity to Soviet propaganda. I am convinced that the American people do not want their athletes cast in that tawdry propaganda charade and I urge you to respect that undeniable consensus."

I watched the Colorado Springs meeting on television in Dublin and found the national emotionalism embarrassing, besides witnessing USOC President Kane subscribing to the boycott that he had previously fought.

Amid that sort of emotive attitude, the vast congregation of sportsmen and sports administrators voted not to go by 1,604 to 797. In view of what was happening in the United States that figure of 797 surprised and delighted me. At least if we were to lose the United States in Moscow there would still be people who could maintain the Olympic cause from a position of loyalty. The resolution by the USOC said that the committee had decided not to send a team to the 1980 Games but gave the opportunity for the president of the United States to advise them on or before May 20 if it was possible to do so.

Besides the individual athletes and the 797 who voted for the Olympic principles, Julian Roosevelt, a member of the IOC for the United States and a former yachting gold medallist, stood out among the administrators appearing on television and writing articles on a worldwide basis. I was delighted when he was elected to the IOC Executive Board in Rome in 1982. William Simon, then a member and now president of the USOC, and a former secretary of the treasury in the Nixon and Ford administrations, supported the boycott, but I have met few American sports administrators who will not admit that Carter's move was a failure.

Twelve days later America was suffering one of the blackest humiliations in its history—the aborted rescue of the hostages in Tehran. In my estimation that failure may have hardened the White House resolve to stop the world going to Moscow and the activity to that end was intensified.

Cyrus Vance resigned from the position of secretary of state after this and I felt deeply sorry for him, for although we had crossed swords at Lake Placid I had always felt him to be a man of integrity.

The USOC decision to boycott brought another danger, and I immediately asked Kane and Miller to appear before the Executive Board at our meeting in Lausanne a week later. Los Angeles had been awarded the Games and was getting anxious that the IOC might react with some disciplinary action that could lead to the Games' being withdrawn from Los Angeles.

The meeting in Lausanne was then going to be crucial. I needed to hear the USOC version of the Colorado withdrawal, discover the strength of support of the IFs, talk with Peter Ueberroth, the Los Angeles organising committee president, and meet with some European NOC members who were working on ideas to "denationalise" the Moscow Games and therefore make it easier for them to participate.

To avoid arousing new alarums I saw Ueberroth at the Intercontinental Hotel in Geneva on April 19 with Monique Berlioux. During the dinner I told him I considered, looking at it from an absolutely neutral point of view, that we had an agreement with Los Angeles, as we had with Moscow, and that this should not be altered for political reasons. He asked for a statement on this, which I gave him, and it was subsequently released to the press. He also mentioned that he understood Kane and Miller might be bringing me a message from Carter and asked if I had any objections. I replied I had none whatsoever and would be quite prepared to receive it sooner if it would be of assistance. He said he would contact the United States and, as a result, on April 21 I received the following message from Carter:

> The position of the United States in opposition to sending a team to the Games of the XXII Olympiad in Moscow results solely from the adverse impact of the Soviet invasion of Afghanistan on the standards of international law and on the preservation of human rights, and on the national security of the United States and many other free world nations. As we advised the USOC, the position of the United States government rests squarely on these grounds. This position does not detract in any way from our belief in the value of the Olympic Movement, our support for the International and National Olympic Committees, and our adherence to the principle that national and international amateur sports should be administered by private bodies and not by governments. We shall continue to oppose the efforts of other governments to establish UNESCO Games, and we shall welcome the IOC and athletes from all eligible Olympic nations at Los Angeles, as we did at Lake Placid.

The USOC appeared before the board at ten in the morning on April 23 to explain its situation. I must admit my own feeling was that prior to Colorado Springs the members of the USOC, individually, had done everything to resist government interference in accordance with our rules, but when it had become a matter of national security they had succumbed to pressures and could be in breach of the Olympic Charter, as our lawyer advised. An NOC must be autonomous and resist pressures of any kind whatsoever of a political, religious, or economic nature.

We told them we would not be making any decisions on the position of the USOC until after the closing date for the Games. There were some who wished to take immediate action against the USOC. The loyal Julian Roosevelt telexed me that he would support the strongest action against the USOC.

The meeting that the international federations held at Lausanne on April 21 and 22, 1980, was positive and brought a tremendous amount of support, but Thomas Keller, who chaired the group as president of the General Assembly of International Federations, spoke to me earlier with some anxiety. Some of the federations were worried that a few IOC members were backtracking from the unanimous Lake Placid statement just at the moment when the NOCs and national federations needed solidarity. I had to agree that there were worries in this area, that Kevan Gosper had voted in Australia for the boycott in spite of his support at Lake Placid, and that reports were coming through that Lance Cross was not being as active in New Zealand as he might. Cross assured me at all times that the matter was being left to each national federation and eventually New Zealand participated, but with only two canoeists. There were reports of opposition from Maurice Herzog in France, besides others.

I assured Keller that I was doing all I could to hold my membership together and that support from the federations at that moment would be a great help.

One surprise in Lausanne was the appearance of Prince Philip, the president of the International Equestrian Federation. He did not always come to these gatherings although he was extremely active in the federation and was meticulous about discharging his responsibilities. His position as a member of the British royal family sometimes caused conflict and embarrassment so I was, frankly, astounded to hear that he had arrived, in view of the attitude of the British government over the Games. I had heard earlier that he was going to attend but assumed there would be a diplomatic withdrawal. Prince Philip has shown his independence on a lot of matters ranging from sport to industry and his views have not always gone down well in his own country. There were reports in the press that he was to make an announcement in Lausanne that he would not be going to Moscow. Other people not in favour of the Games' being held in Moscow inferred that he was going to make a statement against the Moscow Games. The former turned out to be correct, the latter incorrect. The FEI gave the Moscow Games its support, as did all the federations on the programme.

Equestrianism was to suffer most as it was one of the first sports whose Western national federations, led by those of Germany and Switzerland, followed by France, Belgium, and Holland, decided not to participate. This led to others, who wished to compete, also saying no—not on political grounds but on the grounds that the competitions would not be of a high enough standard to justify the expense of the journey to Moscow. This was the sort of domino effect that, of course, was the greatest danger in all the debate. I knew that if one or two important European NOCs decided to withdraw, then many others would fall with them.

Prince Philip joined the federation meeting on its second day and we lunched at the same table. In his conversation with other people at the table some of them formed the impression that he was opposed to the boycott, and that view got through to some reporters.

Keller held a press conference to announce that all the international federations would be present at the 1980 Games to ensure the best possible technical arrangements. Then, in elaborating on the text, he said, "Our role is not a national one; we are an international body with representatives from all parts of the world and it took quite an effort to get a text approved by everyone. A lot of people collaborated in this text and the finishing touches were even made by Prince Philip."

At that moment I could feel a movement among the reporters and realised that it was the British moving swiftly to the telephones. Here indeed was a story; the early editions of the English papers the next day had large headlines such as PHILIP RAPS MAGGIE—which is the interpretation I, as a newspaperman, would have put on the events of Lausanne that day.

What followed, however, was one of the most appalling instances of news manipulation I have known. Ian Wooldridge of the *Daily Mail*, a reporter with a perceptive eye and entertaining style of writing, in addition to hearing what Keller said at the press conference had, in fact, spoken to Prince Philip as he was walking along the main hall of the Lausanne Palace Hotel, when he confirmed that he had taken a hand in wording the statement. That was the nub of Wooldridge's story, which, of course, was directly opposed to the Carter-Thatcher boycott line that the *Mail* editorial board was supporting strenuously.

In the edition that reached Lausanne the following morning, the first off the press, the paper carried the story, leading the front page to the effect that Prince Philip had been involved in a move to support the IOC. By the middle of the morning Wooldridge had a phone call from his deputy sports editor, who, apologetically and with evident embarrassment, read over the story to Wooldridge, which had been altered by some of his colleagues and which was entirely different to the one Wooldridge had sent. It was to the effect that "Buckingham Palace last night denied that Prince Philip . . ." That indicated to the readers of the *Mail* that an earlier story, which they would not have read unless by chance they saw the first edition of the paper, was either inaccurate or a distortion on the writer's part.

A furious Wooldridge spoke over the telephone to Keller and Charles Palmer, the secretary of GAIF, who both confirmed that Prince Philip had taken part in the drafting. Wooldridge therefore wrote another story substantiating his contribution of the previous day, which had appeared in only one edition; the rewrite was not printed. Wooldridge and his sports editor, Tom Clarke, who supported him to the hilt, were both close to resigning.

Throughout my presidency I always had the greatest support from Prince Philip and the FEI and had many useful discussions with him on Olympic matters—whether about the doping of horses or amateur status. He held the same views as I that sport should not be a tool for the use of politicians, and I am sure was quite unaware of what was going on in the corridors of power as he returned to London from Lausanne.

Before he left Lausanne Prince Philip did say to his fellow federation members that he would not find it possible to go to Moscow, which everybody understood, but I have no doubt in my mind that he wanted to go as the head of his sport to perform the duties incumbent on the president of an international federation, as he had done in Montreal.

The meeting in Lausanne also produced some helpful support from the European NOCs. They had already realised that if they supported the Games there were going to be many problems of protocol and ceremonial and these had been studied carefully. It was made clear that the Italian national flag belonged to the Italian government, and while the government might not prevent its citizens from competing (other than state employees), it could prohibit the use of the flag outside the country. With my long-term hope of denationalising the Games, this was one of the few plus points that arose from the dismal affair of the boycott.

It was agreed that each NOC could use its own name rather than its country's name. This was within the rules as amended at Lake Placid, which also permitted using the flag of the NOC or, if there was none, the official flag of the IOC. There is no requirement for anybody to parade at the opening or closing ceremony other than one person to carry the selected flag. In the victory ceremonies, either the national flag, the flag of the NOC, or the Olympic flag could be flown, and the Olympic hymn could be played instead of the national anthem.

This use of the Olympic flag might have been construed as a political demonstration, but it was within the revised charter and part of an effort to denationalise the Games. It was successful. There is no doubt that certain NOCs felt that to dip the national flag to the secretary of a political party, who also happened to be the head of state, would be paying respect to a regime and its politics. I do not consider this to be the case, as wherever I go I accept that it is the right of that country to have whatever form of constitution it chooses, but it does confirm my opinion that the Games should be opened by the president of the IOC in future and not by the head of a political state. The Games belong to the IOC.

A development that came out of the situation was that the NOCs became more united in support of the interests of the future of the Olympic Movement and sport. This unity has remained and I believe will be one of the most important features in the Olympic Movement in the years ahead. In times of trouble they found unity round the table.

One of the proposed changes in the Olympic Movement that I had hoped for had to be abandoned. I always felt it was wrong to elect the IOC president at the time of the Games with so much else to preoccupy members, so I had earlier agreed to stand for two further four-year terms after my initial eight-year term and then resign, in order to start an eight-year cycle from a new point. But I realised as time went by and the boycott campaign was fanned round the world that the number of members who had supported my statement in Lake Placid might diminish when it came to going to Moscow for the IOC session, so the incentive of the election of a new president there would help. One member, Count de Beaumont, now actually suggested that we move the session of the IOC from Moscow, which I thought was an unusual way of demonstrating one's support for the athletes.

One of the areas of protocol and ceremony that worried me was in the use of flash cards at the opening ceremony to make pictures and slogans. These cards can be manipulated to make all types of pictures and diagrams, besides written messages. The word "peace" was going to be used according to the script I had received. The Olympic Movement is for peace, but this word, like "amateur," has become debased. An amateur is considered "not very good" and the word "peace" has been purloined and misused by parties of the left as if they alone wished for peace. The organising committee agreed to alterations or modifications of messages within the rules that were suggested.

Another item of protocol that gave rise to discussion was the famous 1922 Antwerp Olympic flag, which had to be handed over from Montreal to Moscow. Mayor Drapeau, ever loyal to the Olympic Movement, was anxious to be present himself and had not supported the boycott. However, political pressures forbade him to come to Moscow and the Antwerp flag was brought by two torch bearers, who had lit the flame in the main stadium in Montreal.

Prime Minister Trudeau had been returned to power at Christmas, and I believe he would not have maintained the boycott if Canada had not been split politically. But in the event, the Canadians decided not to compete, despite the efforts of the president of the Canadian NOC, Richard Pound, and James Worrall, a former president, both members of the

IOC. It was not only the government pressure that may have had an effect on the way members voted, but the strong economic pressures that arose in several capitalist states. The Canadian Olympic Association is funded by an Olympic trust, which is controlled by experienced businessmen and fund raisers. If they cut off this money the Canadians could not attend, and this is what happened.

In other countries the governments withdrew their subsidies or partial subsidies; for this reason, after consultation, it was agreed that a grant should be given from Olympic Solidarity funds to NOCs wishing to attend the Moscow Games. The amounts of this grant were based on distance from Moscow and made a difference to the NOCs, many of which did not have large financial resources. The Soviets offered assistance but it was pointed out that this might be looked at as buying competitors. Many of the NOCs preferred to make their own arrangements, even if they had to go into debt.

A bad habit had crept in at the time of Munich, and possibly before, when certain countries were subsidised to attend the Games. Prior to Afghanistan the Soviets had always said they would do this for certain Third World delegations. They had asked Olympic Solidarity to assist certain NOCs to travel to airports where Aeroflot had pickup rights, then they would be flown to Moscow free. At the time of the Moscow Games, this proposal was misquoted and misused by political sections of the Western press as if it were a last-minute decision to try to save the Games. I do not believe any NOC received subsidies from Moscow unless they had agreed to assistance prior to the Afghanistan situation. We did agree there could be further assistance in what is always subsidised, accommodation in the Olympic Village.

During this time I was particularly conscious of what was appearing in the British press. Certain reporters found every sort of excuse to make personal attacks on those people who were trying to keep the Olympic Games from the political battlefields. It was these double standards that sickened most of us during this time and it is this that we will long remember— trade and commerce with the Soviet Union but no Olympic Games in Moscow.

Serious papers, such as *The Economist* (which I had treated as a bible and which had strongly supported me two years previously when I had spoken out against ultranationalism and flags), suddenly took a great interest in the Olympic Games, attacking the IOC and, naturally, its president, as being completely out of touch with the world and its realities. I have no objection to anyone's personal opinions on any matter based on fact, but it did strike me that many of the articles on the Olympic Games bore no relationship to the facts. The attacks in the *Daily Telegraph* and *Daily Mail*, which are extremely conservative, were predictable. As one could guess which sports might suffer from the boycott, so one was able to predict which papers in which countries would be for or against the Games, depending on their politics. The Olympic news had left the sporting pages for the political and diplomatic pages.

At this time, comparisons were widely made in the press between Moscow and the Berlin Games of 1936, which took place under the Nazi regime. In my view, the two situations were quite different, and in any case to claim that the 1936 Games made conditions in Germany worse is wrong. Rather the opposite, for the fact that the Games were in Germany drew the world's attention to events there, with independent newsmen on hand to refute the Nazi propaganda.

While there was cohesion among all IFs and many NOCs in regard to Moscow, this was not true of the Western governments, which all had different views. For instance, the president of France and the prime minister of Denmark remained silent. The prime minister of Ireland made a statement against participation but left it up to the NOC to decide whether it would go or not. In the case of Ireland, as opposed to that of Italy, state employees and those in semistate bodies had permission to compete in Moscow. In Ireland this included members of the Defence Forces and Irish Civic Guards and, incidentally, a member of the Royal Ulster Constabulary who was qualified as an Irishman to be on the Irish team. At such times of challenge this form of collaboration shows the true Olympic spirit, which is so largely lacking in any other activities in the world.

After Lake Placid I was holidaying in the South of France when my secretary rang me to say that a newspaper reporter had been in touch with her asking about my membership of a

Lloyd's insurance syndicate. During the debate in the House of Commons on the British participation in the Games, Toby Jessel asked whether members of the IOC had to declare any interests they had. This was inspired by his discovery that a syndicate to which I belong at Lloyd's had underwritten part of the guarantee of the appearance of the United States in the Games in regard to the television rights.

I only hope that members of Parliament are better informed on other facts. No member of Lloyd's knows, unless he is a working member, what he or she is underwriting; power is given completely to the agents and underwriters. The *Daily Telegraph* had heard this story a few months earlier and realised it was a nonstarter, but it was now revived by Jessel and subsequently used in a magazine article. The inference was that I would be influenced as to whether the Games would go ahead in Moscow because of a personal investment. This mention in the House of Commons was the first knowledge I had had of the syndicate's having such an interest and I made enquiries. I was told that Lloyd's had been approached and that the position had been clearly explained to the enquirers from the press. The magazine did correct the article by printing a letter from me. Even had I known about the syndicate's interest, the eventual loss of fifty pounds would not have affected me. This did not give me any sleepless nights, but I did have a feeling of anger at what politicians can do when they get nasty and try to score political points.

When elected president of the IOC I took great care that I would at no time have any business conflicts. I resigned from the board of an Irish company, SSIH, which is associated with Swiss Timing, the official Olympic timekeeper, and also from an investment company that had purchased a leading British gymnastic-equipment-manufacturing concern. I am often asked whether I benefited from being the president of the IOC. There is no doubt that being known in the world has its advantages and disadvantages, but from an economic point of view it was a considerable restraint. In my curriculum vitae I had always declared and listed all my interests, including my membership of Lloyd's.

There is no doubt that all the tensions and pressures left

some scars and divisions in certain NOCs, but I believe these were less than the unity that was created for the future. The Games went ahead as planned, although not with the number of competitors originally thought possible. It was the principle for which the IOC fought and it is for this reason I regret there were one or two members who weakened after Lake Placid. These were correctly subject to criticism by the IFs and NOCs that supported the IOC. NOC Presidents Franco Carraro of Italy, Claud Collard of France, and Raoul Mollet of Belgium were of great assistance, as were Adrian Paulen of the IAAF, Javier Ostos of the swimming federation, and many others.

In Britain virtually all sportswriters, except for one or two specialists in certain sports, were in favour of the Games' going ahead as planned. This was also the view of the sports editors of the international agencies who advised the IOC Press Commission, together with representatives of the other media.

The pressures were not only on those concerned with administering the Games but also on certain other media. Members of the staff of the BBC and some associated with the Independent television stations have told me that although nothing was ever put in writing officially, it was discreetly leaked that the BBC would be looking for increased television fees and that the Independent stations' franchises were due for renewal in 1981—political decisions.

The eventual television coverage of the Moscow Games varied from country to country, some having very full coverage, others only small items in the news bulletins, depending on the control of the television service and the discretion of the management concerned. My correspondence subsequent to the Games seems to confirm they were widely seen, especially the highlights like the opening and closing ceremonies.

The mid-April Lausanne gathering of the various component parts of the Olympic Movement had certainly shored up our position. The next crucial step would be a meeting of European NOCs. The USOC, meanwhile, and the British government had learned one lesson, that alternative Games were not possible. So the Americans shifted all their weight to boycott or postponement, but even towards the end of April their hopes in the direction of the former were beginning to falter.

My next move was to see Brezhnev and Carter. I never expected that I was going to stop a war or bring an about-turn by
an American president, but I felt that I had to follow up what
the IOC had decided in Lake Placid, and the support we had
received subsequently. I sent a telex to Brezhnev on April 23,
1980, suggesting a meeting and received an immediate reply.
The meeting was arranged at the Kremlin for the morning of
May 7. Carter received a telex on the same day as Brezhnev,
and Cutler contacted me saying that in principle a meeting was
agreed but as the president was now pursuing his election campaign his schedule was unsettled. Of course this was just before
the debacle of the failure to release the hostages in Iran. Cutler
wished to come over to Dublin again to discuss the arrangements for the meeting; I could not think why that should have
been necessary.

Just before I went to Moscow the European NOCs had
their third meeting and agreed on the criteria under which they
would participate. Their detailed formula countered the boycott, but made it quite apparent that they were unhappy about
what was going on in Afghanistan. Some announced they would
not participate in the opening ceremony and that only a flag
bearer would follow their name board; they would use the
Olympic flag and the anthem for all ceremonies; they would
confine their activities to sporting events (no receptions or parties) and they asked the IOC to ensure that formal speeches
would have no political content; they would not take part in the
youth camp. It was a brave attempt to keep off the political fir-
ing line of the dispute and to help governments to leave them to
their own individual decisions. The organising committee in
Moscow, which had been party to some of the deliberations, accepted them as there really was no alternative. Clearly, though,
the spectacle of the opening ceremony was going to be spoiled
and whatever the cameras might be doing there could be no
disguising that a lot of competitors and national flags would be
missing.

This part of the declaration was carried out, but the second, of equal importance in my opinion, was not. It said: "In
conclusion, after 1980 the NOCs can no longer accept, either
for the athletes or the Olympic Movement, a continuation of

the difficulties which we are experiencing at this time. Consequently they consider it of paramount importance that the whole of the Olympic Movement instigates an immediate examination with a view to changing the basic concept of the Olympic Games. These changes should be designed to eliminate political pressures and all types of exploitation and give the Olympic Movement a new impetus and the necessary authority for survival." Idealistic perhaps, but it seemed to me like a sound base for discussion after the Games. It was, though, along with other suggestions, swept under the carpet, except for an approach to the politically motivated United Nations.

I decided to take Monique Berlioux to Moscow and Washington. I felt it was best to have an executive rather than an IOC member. She has a vast technical knowledge and a good memory, and would be the best adviser. When I told her of my decision she was surprised. "Do you want to make me more unpopular with some of your members than I already am?" she asked, a reference to the fact that some people believed she was too dictatorial in the way she carried out her duties.

We arrived in Moscow late on May 6, where we were met on the tarmac by Novikov and Smirnov. I proceeded with Novikov to the house that I had stayed in previously in the Lenin Hills. This is one of a series of houses in luxurious gardens built by Stalin for the Presidium. Subsequently they were only used for visiting heads of state. This one had a large staff and luxurious furnishings. The rooms were spacious, as indeed were the baths and all the fittings. Though Soviets do not wear black tie for the ballet or receptions, white shirts are customary. When, on earlier visits, I would change my coloured day shirt, I would find it on the bed impeccably laundered when returning a few hours later after the entertainment—even with a cardboard bow tie to keep the collar in position. As I recollect, the domestic staff included several butlers, a chef, and kitchen staff, besides housemaids. The comfort and luxury were ancien régime, the architecture Stalinesque.

Novikov, I thought, was rather ill at ease and worried. I told him, as I subsequently informed the president of the Soviet Union, that it was very unlikely many of the Western European NOCs would accept the invitation to the Games and my estimate was a maximum of 50. The organising committee had originally hoped for over 120, while I had felt we would have somewhere around the 100-minus mark even under normal conditions. There are many NOCs that do not have athletes of Olympic standard but have created NOCs partly for prestige, and to assist in developing sport. It is these we try to help with the Olympic Solidarity fund.

At eleven the next morning we left for the Kremlin, passing through the main gate and the building where I had met Brezhnev on my first visit to Moscow. We drew up at the door that I had entered on previous occasions when visiting Kosygin and Podgorny. We were ushered upstairs, waited for a few minutes in the anteroom, and were then shown into President Brezhnev's room. He was standing to greet us and welcomed me in a friendly way with smiles. It was a difficult moment as I naturally have a slightly nervous smile when I meet people and I wished to appear as serious as possible. Unfortunately the photographs did not confirm this. After being televised and photographed we proceeded to the conference table. At the end of the table was an interpreter, whose English was impeccable. Brezhnev sat opposite me; beside him, Novikov, an adviser named Blatov, and Smirnov. I had a feeling all the time that Novikov and Smirnov were somewhat overawed by the presence of the president and, more important, the first secretary of the Communist party. Berlioux sat on my right and we proceeded to a formal welcome.

Then, as if ignoring the United States, Brezhnev said that it was important for other nations, such as West Germany, France, and Spain, to take part. He, like myself, felt whatever West Germany did, the rest of Western Europe would follow. He told me he was leaving that night for President Tito's funeral in Yugoslavia, where he hoped to have a word with Chancellor Helmut Schmidt of West Germany. His requests were to be that pressure should not be put by Schmidt's government on the West German NOC so the athletes could take part in the Games. It was then over to me. After the courtesy of thanking him for his speech I said I was anxious to put myself at anyone's disposal in order to assist the situation. I stressed that from the beginning, whatever my personal feelings were, as president of the IOC I was neutral and above politics. As I was not convinced the Soviets had not at times used the Games for political kudos, I stressed my concern that the Games should not be used for political purposes. Referring to my letter of February 14 asking that the Games be held in the right atmosphere, I quoted from the reply I had received via Novikov, which rather simplistically laid all the blame for the Games' present difficulties at President Carter's feet. I said I would not go into the Afghanistan situation but, as President Brezhnev had given me an opening, I was wondering if he could make a statement in the early future in order to release the international tension.

I explained that one of the weapons used by the United States and its allies was the booklet entitled *Handbook for Party Activists*, published well before Afghanistan by the Soviet Communist party, of which, of course, Brezhnev was first secretary. I could not read the original but had received a copy of the translation that had been circulated through all diplomatic channels. The handbook was harmless and generally in praise of the Olympic Movement, but it did contain this paragraph, which I read to Brezhnev: "The decision to give the honoured right to hold the Olympic Games to the capital of the world's first socialist state has become convincing testimony of the general recognition of the historical importance and correctness of the foreign political course of our country with the enormous service of the Soviet Union in the struggle for peace and the contribution to the International Olympic Movement to the development of physical culture and sports." This I had heard quoted by Malcolm Fraser on British television when he was in London, as well as by Cyrus Vance at Lake Placid, and it had probably done more damage than any other tool used by those opposed to holding the Games in Moscow.

As I was quoting, this was being translated from my English back into Russian, and Brezhnev interrupted saying, "What's wrong with that?" I replied that to my mind everything was wrong, for the Games were awarded to Moscow not on political grounds but on the ability of Moscow to stage the Games in the proper way. Novikov then interrupted to stress that the booklet was an internal document for the Soviets' own work inside their party. He affirmed that he had never set eyes on the booklet and it was only a minor problem.

The discussion then reverted to the question of Chancellor

Schmidt's leaving his national Olympic committee alone to make up its own mind. Most of the Western European NOCs wished to take part, and I pointed out that certain NOCs are completely independent from their government and felt it was their duty to enable their athletes to take part in the Games anywhere in the world. The danger would be that if West Germany said no and its NOC agreed, it would snowball. Furthermore, some national federations had decided that even if their NOC said yes, they would say no. This was particularly true of yachting and equestrianism and it could have an effect on other competitions, which might not be of the usual high standard. I stressed as best I could how critical the situation was and reminded Brezhnev that when Moscow had been awarded the Games the choice was welcomed by at least 90 percent of people around the world. That had been the time of detente but now it appeared to be approaching a time of cold war again.

Finally, I asked Brezhnev to do everything in his power to help in the interests of sport and the organising committee, which had worked so hard for sportsmen, and I made a final appeal to him to do something about Afghanistan to avoid the political destruction of the Games. I told him the Olympic Movement, which enables people with various differing ideas and ideologies to meet under the Olympic banner, had to be saved. He gave me a promise to do his very best so that the atmosphere might improve.

During our talk, which was very frank, the telephone rang twice. There were batteries of telephones on Brezhnev's right and I noticed that he was slow on his feet and somewhat clumsy with his hands. On one call he obviously said he was in conference with me and I don't know what the other was about. What flashed through my mind was how terrifying it was that this gentleman, who was certainly mentally very alert but physically not so well, could pick up a telephone and set off a world war. Brezhnev was covered with decorations, which he does not wear all the time, because he was leaving immediately afterwards for Tito's funeral.

The meeting lasted over an hour. Afterwards Novikov was very anxious I should visit the organising committee but, again, I did not want to give unnecessary publicity in Moscow other than a short press release. I noticed that two of the people with whom I had conversations interrupted me, suggesting that the room was either warm or stuffy and that it would be a good idea to walk in the garden. I still wonder whether this was because all the conversations were being monitored. Many stories of so-called bugging in the Soviet Union may be exaggerated, especially as far as the casual visitor is concerned, but there is no doubt at all everyone is watched and monitored, as I believe I was in Washington and Lake Placid.

There were many offers and requests that I should stay on for a few days and inspect the sites, but I was intent on not being used for any form of Soviet propaganda. My only loyalty was to the Olympic Games, to endeavour to ensure the maximum number of participants in the Games in accordance with the rules. I also made it clear again that I would not give a press conference before I had visited Washington, the date of which had not been finally fixed.

After my return to Dublin, Lloyd Cutler came immediately from Washington to see me as arranged. I think he was agitated at the possibility that I was going to play Brezhnev versus Carter and vice versa. We went through the tiresome discussion yet again about postponing or cancelling the Games and he informed me, with a brave attempt to put authority into his voice, that West Germany was about to withdraw (which turned out to be correct) and the rest of Europe would collapse too (which was not). As in the case of the United States, the Germans were on a run-up to an election and that had a material effect.

At least we did not mention alternative Games. It seemed barely credible that up to two weeks before he and David Wolper, a film producer, had been in Lausanne trying to organise alternative Games, much to the embarrassment of the Los Angeles organising committee for 1984, of which Wolper was a member. Cutler showed some anxiety about the possibility of the IOC, or ultimately the Soviet Union, accepting individual entries, but the IOC had looked at this proposal before and unfortunately found it too complicated to implement.

As our discussions continued I frequently wondered whether it was worthwhile even bothering to see President

Carter, who, from what Cutler was telling me, seemed to have rigid ideas and had put himself in a position from which there was nowhere to withdraw, but I felt it was essential to go through with the trip, and May 16 was the day arranged.

Berlioux met me in London and we flew to Washington by Concorde. We were booked under my name, Michael Morris, and her married name, Mme. Serge Groussard. The British Airways officials recognised me but paid no attention. We were met by a car at the airport and had been booked into the Madison Hotel under our travelling names as we did not want to be bombarded by the press. I rang Cutler immediately and he confirmed that we should be at the White House around eleven the next morning for a meeting at eleven-thirty.

Cutler told me when we arrived that, strangely enough, people did not take notes during meetings with the president of the United States, unlike meetings at the Kremlin, and I warned the director of this.

It was not until this occasion that I realised Cutler was a powerful man behind a weak president. He introduced me to the many secretaries and advisers and the assistant in his office. He said we would go and meet the president in the Oval Office. Just as we were leaving I heard him say, "I think we should invite [National Security Adviser] Brzezinski and [Deputy Secretary of State] Warren Christopher as well." It appeared it was Cutler who had decided who should be present when I saw the president, and not the president himself.

A common feature of the Kremlin and the White House was the long queues of people waiting either to enter or to pass by. In both places they were not people from the capital, but provincial sightseers of many different ethnic groups. The noticeable difference was that in the Soviet Union there were fewer people of African origin, as the slaves and serfs in the czars' times came from among their own people.

We were shown into the study where Carter was standing. He could not have been more courteous, smiling, or friendly. He reassured me of his interest in the Olympic Movement. We sat down and started our conversation before the arrival of Zbigniew Brzezinski, Carter reiterating that the United States government's position resulted from the Soviet invasion of Afghanistan. He stressed that this position did not detract in any way from the support of the Olympic Movement, and that his government was looking forward to the 1984 Games in Sarajevo and Los Angeles, and would do its best to help heal any scars created by these events. He told me of steps to increase the financial support for the USOC so that it might be able to continue to remain an important force in the Olympic Movement. (It has, of course, been suggested that this promised long-term financial support eventually swayed the USOC, which earlier had been so firm in supporting the attendance of American athletes in Moscow and Los Angeles.) He was so anxious for a postponement of the Olympic Games and had obviously been informed by Cutler that this was impossible. The situation in Afghanistan was unchanged and the postponement would have made no difference even if it had been feasible.

Carter asked my advice and counsel regarding the strengthening of the Olympic Movement and raised the question of a permanent home in Greece. To give him his due, he fully realised the decision could only be made by the IOC, but said that the United States would be prepared to support it, especially as it had a very large ethnic Greek group. Whatever the eventual recommendations made by the IOC on a permanent site in Greece, one point that must always be borne in mind is that the governments that endeavoured to prevent their athletes competing in Moscow were among the greatest supporters of a permanent site in Greece, e.g., the United States, Britain, and West Germany. This created a diversion.

I reiterated our position and said there was no way of reneging on the contract with Moscow. I pointed out that it was not compulsory for any NOC to accept an invitation to go to the Games and that I had personally not interfered with the decision of a single NOC. However, we were opposed to individual entries. Our only wish was to strengthen and give freedom of action to the NOCs, without governmental pressures. The United States authorities had stated that virtually no United States citizen could attend either the Games or the events that surround the Games, such as the meetings of the international federations. Had this been implemented, it would have meant that there would have been no United States, or possibly allied, representatives at the congresses of the various IFs, and if the West wished to hand over everything to the East, this was the best way of doing it. The same applied to the press, and the president assured me that the American international federation delegates and press would be permitted to go to Moscow. Berlioux raised the question of NBC, which had the exclusive rights for television. Cutler answered that NBC would not televise the Games on an exclusive basis but American television would be permitted to cover the Games on a news basis to the extent permitted by the IOC.

I described the salient points that had arisen with Brezhnev. We had not, as reported in the press, discussed denationalisation, but had been assured that the organising committee would abide by any rule or instructions given by the IOC, such as the rule permitting Olympic committees to parade with their own NOC flag or under the IOC flag. The president asked me, somewhat naïvely I thought, what he could do to help the Olympic Movement in the next few weeks. I replied that the most helpful thing he could do was for the American athletes to be allowed to go to the Moscow competitions. At this moment the president's smile vanished for a second, and he replied that of course this was not possible.

We got up to leave the room and the president asked me the length of my term of office. I told him I had been elected for eight years and that I was not offering myself for reelection. To this the president replied, with the pending election, "I wish I was elected for eight years." I said smilingly that it was a pity that his constitution could not be changed so that the primary and presidential elections did not coincide with the Olympic Games, as will happen again in Los Angeles in 1984.

As a last point, I asked whether it was possible for Los Angeles to be declared an international zone for the three weeks of the Olympic Games, but Carter replied that it created problems, such as the handling of security.

I met the press on the White House steps. Obviously the White House press corps is politically oriented, but in spite of all that had been written about the Olympic Games in the past few months I was asked a large number of ignorant questions again about cancelling the Games and alternate Games, as well as being asked what I would do if this were 1940 and the Games were being held in Germany. In 1940, of course, a world war had been in progress, which was hardly the case now. (Some cynical journalists have written that the United States was late for two wars and is therefore anxious to be early for the next one.) The long and short of it, I explained, was that I had been to see President Carter, and I had also seen President Brezhnev the previous week, and the IOC position remained unchanged: the Games would go on even if I had to compete alone against myself, because we had an agreement with Moscow.

Looking back on these two visits to the two men who held the most important posts on earth, I have great anxiety for the future of the world. On the one hand there is Soviet bureaucracy and all I dislike in the Communist system, or any authoritarian and bureaucratic system, but it seems to me difficult for the free world to be led effectively by the United States. The election of the president as chief executive and head of state for a short term of four years gives him about one year to carry out his promised policy as far as he can, and then he starts looking over his shoulder, not towards the opposition party but towards the opposition within his own party at the coming primaries. The more I look back the more it is extraordinary that a vast country like the United States could not produce a greater leader or statesman than Carter.

On the day I went to Washington we lost the support of our most important European NOC, West Germany's. Again the whole affair was orchestrated in a manner that indicated the influence of the United States. The NOC arranged to have a meeting in Düsseldorf, and the day before West German President Karl Carstens invited all those taking part to a reception to give them the country's position. Then, when the delegates arrived the following morning for their crucial debate, not only did they find it was in public with the press present, but it was televised live, like a congressional committee hearing. There are strong arguments for open debate and almost as strong arguments for private discussion, but here, I would suggest, was subtle ploy to weigh the argument heavily against the Olympic cause. The heads of federations needed to talk privately with one another to search out each other's views rather than stand up and speak to the nation. The debate was not about a nation or nationalism, it was about the Olympic Movement. When I heard that the vote to boycott had carried in those circumstances, by 59 to 40, I did wonder what the outcome might have been had the meeting been in private and the IOC position put by someone in an independent position, such as Monique Berlioux.

In Australia the struggle went on to the eleventh hour with Prime Minister Fraser exhorting the sportsmen to stay at home. In the end, by one vote, Australia competed. In Japan seven national federations wished to take part in the Games individually, and the IOC Executive Board agreed that if the NOC was prepared to sign the entry they would be accepted. The Japanese NOC president in due course found this impossible without splitting his committee.

The deadline for accepting invitations from the organising committee was May 24. I was in Dublin when a call came from the IOC headquarters telling me that the total of acceptances was seventy-nine (later revised to eighty-one). Having believed three weeks previously that we might not get more than fifty, I was, in a way, delighted. The Olympic world had stood up magnificently to the power of the United States and its political friends. Neither side had scored a victory—Carter certainly had not succeeded—but without many of the world's outstanding competitors the Games would in some areas be devalued. The boycott seemed pointless at that moment in May, and has become more so with Afghanistan resuming the obscurity it has always suffered, except when rebels were giving trouble. It was ironic that when the British were winning Olympic medals in 1924, their troops were trying to put down rebels in Afghanistan.

When the Executive Board met again in June to review the situation, it was decided that the media accreditation allocation should be halved for those countries not attending the Games. The Americans meanwhile (and some other countries) began changing their personnel, the sportswriters being replaced by political columnists. Even the *Guardian* put in a Kremlinologist on an Olympic accreditation. Strictly speaking all these people could have been rejected under the rules, and as far as the Americans who applied were concerned they could have been turned down due to late applications, because of the time it takes to process visas. The Press Commission pressed for the Americans' acceptance and I took the view that with so much Olympic misunderstanding in the United States, anyone would be better than no one.

The Games themselves were joyless. Too often we were thinking of the missing people, wondering and weighing up what might have happened.

Moscow today is a city of great contrasts, with its Stalin-esque architecture and heavy, wedding-cake minarets and towers that dominate part of the city, and its new streets, such as Kalinin Prospekt, with its glass-fronted, panelled shops and ever-increasing number of consumer goods, which could be anywhere in the world. The average tourist is very critical but I find this unfair. Some of the quality is shoddy and the privileged people in the upper echelons of the Soviet system have special shops, as do those with foreign currency to spare, whether they be diplomats or tourists. However, the folk art designs are quite excellent and it is only some of the more modern designs that are somewhat "old-fashioned." The Moscow of 1980, in fact, was a very different Moscow to the one I had first visited. The women were now smartly dressed. The service in the hotels (although with VIP treatment I suppose we were not always in a position to judge) had changed beyond recognition. Eighteen years previously a waiter had been considered a form of serf, which, combined with the bureaucracy of form filling and the difficulty of ordering dishes by number and not being certain of what one was going to be served, made tourists complain bitterly because the meals took so long to appear. In those days, I confined myself to caviare and ice cream, but this can be a very tedious diet for a fortnight.

The security for visitors was oppressive: electronic checks were made at the main hotels housing the overseas officials, media, and so on, which of course was necessary, but the screening of visitors was unusual. If anyone wanted to visit a foreign guest in his hotel he had to go to a kiosk just outside and give his name and address and the name of the person he wanted to see. Thus there was a record of any liaison or link between a Soviet citizen and someone from overseas.

I still hold the belief, however, that without the boycott and with three or four hundred thousand foreign visitors, the long, slow process of accommodation between Communist Europe and Western society would have been helped in some small way by the Games. I felt, too, in my dealings with Soviet officials with whom I worked over the years, that they really wanted that to happen. The younger ones, when they grow older, may not have such strong views about the Western world and capitalism, because unlike their fathers and grandfathers they will not remember the czarist days or the postrevolution years. It is a small hope to which I cling in this mad world.

There were, of course, reminders of the boycott. Some IOC members came to the session and departed before the Games started because their teams were not taking part. I missed people like Worrall, Pound, Beaumont, Jean of Luxembourg, and others.

Berthold Beitz, who was against the boycott, scored his own unwitting triumph. A keen sailor, he took his yacht *Germania VI* into Tallinn, where a decimated Olympic competition was to take place. He brought the ship into the new Olympic facilities and it happened to be positioned so that the West German national flag was visible during the opening ceremony there. I suppose the Soviets might think this was a political coup, but I know he chuckles about the event now.

Shortly before the Games it was suggested to me that since the Americans had gone through the process of selecting their Olympic athletes and issuing them with the appropriate certificate and kit, these athletes were authentic Olympic competitors and could perfectly well take part in the Games. Some of them were competing in Europe and would therefore have no difficulty getting into the Soviet Union. The temptation was strong, not to score a point over Carter, but because I knew that there was a fierce desire among some American competitors to take part. However, I believed that had this been allowed to happen, the reputations and careers of those Americans who came to Moscow would have been in danger.

In a similar spirit of concern for the athletes, the Olympic Movement, and the larger purposes it serves, I closed the Moscow Games—mutilated though they had been by politicians, leaving torment, anguish, and remorse where there should have been friendship and greater international understanding to match the pinnacles of sporting achievement. At the final ceremony, in one of my last acts as president of the IOC, I said in part, "I implore the sportsmen of the world to unite in peace before the holocaust descends. . . . The Olympic Games are for the benefit of our children."

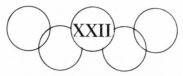

Sitting Back in Dublin

My eight years as IOC president were unquestionably the most difficult the Olympic Movement has experienced to date. The boycott of the Moscow Games was the most damaging event since the Games were revived in 1896. The more I look back on the year of 1980, the more I realise that but for the support of the West European countries, such as Belgium, Britain, Denmark, France, Ireland, Italy, Holland, Spain, Sweden, and Switzerland, together with Australia and New Zealand, among others, the Olympic Games would now be something of the past. Therefore I regret that the IOC did not make a closer analysis of all the events that occurred between the Soviet Union's occupation of Afghanistan and the opening of the Games in Moscow, which I recommended. The attitude of the IOC that bygones should be bygones and that everything should be swept under the carpet is dangerous. It is wrong to take the easy course.

When my term of office came to an end in 1980, I think I ought to have made some reference, perhaps a plea, at the congress in Baden-Baden that the boycott was indeed a subject for enquiry, in order that we might learn from the experience. However, I was conscious of the fact that I might be tarred with the same brush as my predecessor and be accused of interfering, as I was no longer a member of the IOC. Yet I made an error in not speaking out and so encouraging the new president and his members to look over their shoulders. Efforts to prevent another boycott are being made by way of a UN Resolution, but I have my reservations as this might ultimately result in counter-resolutions and is asking a political body to interfere.

After the Montreal walkout by twenty-two countries, mostly African, because the IOC would not agree to withdrawing New Zealand from the Games, there was a demand for sanctions against the departing nations. The following year the Executive Board asked those countries that had not taken part in the Montreal Games to give their reasons. But even when the questionnaire was sent out I knew that IOC members were getting cold feet about the subject, for many of them, like myself, could see that any sanction we might impose would ultimately affect the athlete. In my eight years as president, and many before that, I had always striven, even at the cost of bending or twisting the rules, to get the competitors into the arena. After all, the athletes come first. Indeed, most of the questionnaires were returned with excuses and there was no follow-up.

This experience after Montreal created an unfortunate precedent for which I take the blame. There was, of course, a world of difference between Montreal and Moscow, although the same word, "boycott," was stamped on both. However, I feel that the IOC should have conducted a similar enquiry in 1981 on a much broader basis and that every NOC should have been given the opportunity to give explanations for not participating.

This would probably have revealed that some IOC members had been influenced by their NOCs and that perhaps even national Olympic committees had taken their attitude from the IOC members. We might have discovered more NOCs whose absence had nothing to do with the boycott. Perhaps too we may have found members with views similar to those of Kevan Gosper, who, at least, was open about his support of the boycott; twice he flew back to Melbourne to support with his vote a move to stop the Australian NOC from attending the Games. He did have qualms of conscience throughout this period and was in contact with me several times. How many other members had views of this kind, whether as strong as Gosper's or not, will never be known, but some remain suspect in my eyes. I make this point because new members of the IOC take an oath of allegiance, which includes abiding by decisions of the IOC;

and the IOC decision was that the Games would proceed in Moscow.

If this sort of enquiry had taken place, then some members in breach of their oath could have been subject to expulsion, while others would have been cleared of all suspicion. This would have strengthened the authority of an organisation that is always being accused (correctly in some cases) of turning a blind eye to competitors who disobey its rules.

Another proposal, which I put forward at the session in Rome in 1982 and which has since been adopted, was that the IOC president should be elected in the year after the Games take place. Had I been in office until 1981 I would have been able to put things in better shape for my successor, including questions about the boycott. Also, I found it embarrassing being president-elect during the Munich Games, as I am sure did my successor and friend Juan Antonio Samaranch in Moscow.

During my term as president of the IOC, I had made our family home in Dublin the tactical headquarters. The basement became an office and sounds reverberated about the house of the tapping of typewriters and the chugging of the telex. My name had been removed from the telephone directory, but this still did not stop people ringing up at all hours, forgetting that when we were fast asleep they were just about to rise in the antipodes.

Every letter or official communication I sent out was addressed as from Lausanne, as it had always been my intention to make it quite clear that the IOC headquarters were there, and copies of any correspondence I sent out from Dublin were sent to the director in Lausanne. This was in order to avoid a repetition of the experiences I had had in the past, when a communication with President Brundage in Chicago was often unknown to the headquarters and members of the Executive Board of the IOC until it appeared in the papers or on radio and television.

My name is now back in the telephone book and there are no calls at unearthly hours. As honorary life president I am consulted as an elder statesman but I will not get involved in any of the day-to-day transactions of the IOC, which are the responsibility of the president or the board and the members. My house is now littered with photographs, souvenirs, medals, and decorations, while the mews at the rear has been turned into a small Olympic museum, and resembles a stall in the Portobello Road or the Marché aux Puces in Paris.

Australia is particularly remembered by a very simple plaque that was presented to me in Moscow by the Australian team. Their NOC insisted on its political freedom to participate in the Games and not come under the influence of Prime Minister Fraser, who had thumped his way through the world on Jimmy Carter's boycott campaign—ill advised, unsuccessful, and only damaging to the athletes and the common interest of sport.

Once, however, I declined a form of recognition. In 1980 I learned that President Brezhnev had gazetted me for the Order of the Friendship of Peoples, which had previously been awarded to the spy Kim Philby. As I considered my services had been to the Olympic Movement and not the Soviet Union as such, I did not accept. I was much happier to receive the Olympic Order at the Baden-Baden congress in 1981.

The walls of my study are covered with photographs of heads of state and people I met, especially during my eight years as president. One photograph of Empress Farah of Iran reminds me of my second visit to Tehran for the Asian Games. The shah had built an Olympic complex, hoping to stage the Games in due course. I was told that as a special honour I could drive to the stadium through the archway reserved for him. When we arrived the gates were locked and the sentry, who obviously had not been advised of our arrival, refused to open it. I was prepared to drive around the normal route, when an officer with a swagger stick hopped out of the first car to reprimand the soldier, who was probably only obeying orders. The next thing he did was to strike the soldier in the face and I thought to myself that when the inevitable change came in the regime, the full support of the Army could not be certain. My Iranian companion tried to distract my attention from the scene.

Olympic people close to the shah assured me that if the Games were given to Tehran there would be no marathon. This seemed to bring into contemporary sports politics a new di-

"It's Lord Killanin seeking a
home for the 1984 Olympics."

DAILY MAIL – JULY 21, 1978

mension, where the defeat of the Persians by the Greeks in 480 B.C. was still a preoccupation. Such a dictate would not have been accepted by the IOC or the IAAF.

I have been cheered by the many cartoons that poked fun at me, especially those by Dero of *L'Équipe* and Osbert Lancaster of the *Daily Express*. One is by Jon of the *Daily Mail* showing the black Olympic ring falling on my head after the African walkout at Montreal. My favourite of Jon's is one of Margaret Thatcher tangled hopelessly in the Olympic rings, which appeared at the time of her efforts to thwart the Moscow Games. Whatever the crisis it has been imperative to laugh.

One of the important questions that have preoccupied me since the late sixties is that of eligibility, or amateur status. We have now moved to a dangerous point. Changes should be made cautiously and I think that because of the complicated IOC-IF relationship, with a sport conducting its own events under its own rules for four years and then having to subscribe to Olympic rules, which may be different, there should be flexibility and, above all, patience in making changes.

With the creation of trust funds into which is placed money earned by athletes from advertising, sponsorship, personal appearances, television, and journalistic work, it is now possible for the competitor to meet all his needs during his competitive days and then finish with a lump sum. A percentage of these monies goes to the national federation. This proposition is an attraction to agents, who take a fee for arranging the life of a personality, trying to organise his publicity and exposure. It is, as from the early days of Hollywood films, developing into a highly sophisticated and, in many areas, respectable business. But there are dangers in the agents and managers influencing, through their competitors, the control of sport.

I wonder whether there may not come a time when a group of athletes, under one management, only compete in the Olympic Games if their agent receives a small (and later large) slice of the television fee. After all, without 1,500-metre runner A against runner B, and without high jumper C, that very attractive Swedish blonde with the shapely legs, will the competition be really worthwhile for television? This sort of control may come, wrapped up in more subtle management agreements and clauses; we must resist it for the sake of the development of the sport at the grass roots. Also, an Olympic gold medal at the time of the competitions is a greater reward than any amount of cash.

My last official speaking appearance was at the congress at Baden-Baden on October 24, 1981. It was my duty to review my eight Olympic years as president and I took as my guidelines the resolutions that had been formulated after the Olympic congress at Varna in 1973.

Until my term of office came to an end, I was very directly involved with the organisation and planning of this congress. I revisited Baden-Baden, and questions of security and the safety of the delegates from the many organisations, in addition to the IOC, IFs, and NOCs, had to be considered. West Germany had been the centre of many anarchist and subversive kidnappings, bombings, and outrages, but Baden-Baden could easily be sealed off, allowing all the delegates to mix freely.

All through my presidential years I had sought to draw attention to the fact that the athletes should take precedence. It was with this in mind that I had asked a number of selected athletes to Varna as observers, and it had been decided they should also be given the floor to express their views at the next congress. Eventually the selection was left to the NOCs, in conjunction with the IFs, which gave the necessary time for speaking. At Baden-Baden we went a step further with a panel of athletes meeting during the congress and contributing to the daily proceedings, culminating in a résumé by the well-educated and articulate British runner Sebastian Coe.

Yet I wonder whether it is correct to short-circuit the normal channels through which athletes should express themselves—their clubs, the national federations, and then the international federations, or the national Olympic committees on Olympic matters. To avoid chaos in sports administration it is important that the correct channels be used. On the other hand, there is no doubt that many members of the IOC, NOCs, and IFs are not in touch with those for whom they administer.

The congress, which was followed by an IOC session, confirmed or completed many of the tasks and ambitions that I had set myself but had been denied to me in view of the extremely difficult circumstances that surrounded the session in Moscow. Many of the ambitions I had said I wished to achieve after my election at Munich were accomplished. For the first time, two women were elected, Flor Isave Fonseca of Venezuela and Pirjo Haggman of Finland, who had been a competitor at Montreal. These were not token women but women who had been selected on their merits.

From the platform I could see the delegates sitting as I had sat as president of an NOC for over twenty years, between the NOCs of Iran or Iraq and Israel, some of which were not overly anxious to sit next door to each other. Israel had had its Olympic problems, not only with the assassinations at Munich, which resulted in a German reaction to endeavour under all circumstances to have a member of the IOC in Israel, but also through their exclusion from the Mediterranean Games and the Asian Games because of Arab influence. While I was looking for a member in Israel, a qualified person, some of the Arabs had pressed me to increase the number of members of the IOC for their countries, which were already well represented. However, I had resisted a premature nomination for Israel as I felt the time was not opportune, with the many problems in the Middle East. Rather than bringing sport above politics one might, by hastiness, aggravate the situation to the detriment of the athletes.

I had also never become officially involved in any games that were confined to an ethnic group (e.g., Maccabi, Arab), religious group (e.g., Maccabi, Catholic), political group (e.g., Commonwealth)—in fact any games that were not open to all people within a geographic area. In this I followed in the steps of Coubertin, who believed in regional games as stepping-stones towards the Olympic Games. In no way was I opposed to these other games, but I felt it was the duty of the IOC not to be involved.

At Baden-Baden the idea of a permanent site for the Games received little support and for the foreseeable future the Games will be allocated by application and selection. The choice for 1988 lay between Seoul, Korea, and Nagoya, Japan.

Candidates for the Winter Games were Calgary, Canada; Cortina d'Ampezzo, Italy; and Falun, Sweden. I was able to hear the presentation but, naturally, no longer being a member of the IOC, did not take part in the session and left immediately after the presentation and before the voting. Surprisingly, Seoul and Calgary were subsequently selected.

Avery Brundage, when congratulating me on my election as his successor, told me that there was no likelihood of the Games' being held in Montreal as the facilities would not be ready. Perhaps Brundage thought that the Games without him were not imaginable. Certainly he would not be happy if he saw many of the changes that have come about since his time, and not all for the better with increasing commercialisation, but changes there must be.

When I handed over the presidency in 1980 to Juan Antonio Samaranch, I told him also that the Games would continue despite problems and stressed the importance of evolution. I made a number of specific suggestions for improvements in the organisation of the Games, several of which he has already implemented while also, of course, introducing ideas of his own. I expect, too, that by now he has discovered another aspect of being president of the International Olympic Committee; as I wrote before the election of my successor, whoever that was to be, "there is one thing of which I can assure you—you will find it very lonely at times."

Glossary

(Some acronyms derive from the organisation's name in French or another language.)

AAU	U.S. Amateur Athletic Union
AIPS	International Sportswriters Association
ANOC	Association of National Olympic Committees
BOA	British Olympic Association, the NOC of Great Britain.
CNOSF	French NOC and sports federation
CONI	Italian NOC
commissions	committees and subcommittees set up by the IOC
congresses	called by the IOC and attended by IOC, IFs, NOCs, and invited interested parties
FEI	International Equestrian Federation
FIFA	International Association Football (soccer) Federation
FIMS	International Federation of Sports Medicine

FINA	International Amateur Swimming Federation
FIS	International Ski Federation
GAIF	General Assembly of International Federations
IAAF	International Amateur Athletic Federation, the governing body of track and field
IF	international federation, an association controlling a particular sport
IOC	International Olympic Committee
IRA	Irish Republican Army
NOC	national Olympic committee, an association recognised by the IOC and responsible for all Olympic matters in a country, territory, or area
Olympiad	period of four successive years following the Games
organising committee	set up to organise the Games by the NOC of the country in which they are to be held
PASO	Pan American Sports Organisation, responsible for the Pan American Games
SANROC	South African Non-Racial Open (or Olympic) Committee, an unofficial body organised to combat apartheid in sport in South Africa
SCSA	Supreme Council for Sport in Africa
session	full meeting of the IOC
UNESCO	United Nations Educational, Scientific, and Cultural Organisation
USOC	United States Olympic Committee

INDEX